BEE

D0930452

20945

PN   Roberts
3331   When is something fiction?
.R6

LIBRARY
BEE COUNTY
COLLEGE

Crosscurrents / MODERN CRITIQUES

Harry T. Moore, *General Editor*

PN 3331 .R6

When
Is Something Fiction?

Thomas J. Roberts

WITH A PREFACE BY
Harry T. Moore

SOUTHERN ILLINOIS UNIVERSITY PRESS
Carbondale and Edwardsville

FEFFER & SIMONS, INC.
London and Amsterdam

20945

LIBRARY
BEE COUNTY
COLLEGE

for Betty

Copyright © 1972 by Southern Illinois University Press
All rights reserved
Printed in the United States of America
Designed by Andor Braun
International Standard Book Number 0–8093–0578–X
Library of Congress Catalog Card Number 79–188698

Contents

Preface

Most of us habitually use the word fiction to mean short stories and novels, always of course written in prose. In the present book, Professor Roberts points out eighteen different ways in which critics use the term. But their treatments of the word often overlap, and do so in a fairly regular if somewhat intricate pattern.

He considers how these operate "along four different axes of meaning," which he explores carefully and valuably. He doesn't concentrate on recent writers, though some of them appear, but ranges over the whole field of what can be labeled fiction, from the Greek epics to Ulysses. There are continuously interesting observations, for example the passages dealing with Gibbon's Decline and Fall of the Roman Empire: political scientists consider it to be history, and literary critics look upon it as literature. As far as history goes, however, the book is "dated," frozen into the incomplete knowledge of its time. It is not "bad" history; it is merely obsolete. But in the realm of literature, even that part of it dealing with fiction, Gibbon's work has a high standing. He intended it as fact—Professor Roberts looks closely into the problems of intentions and values—but it has wound up as what might be called fiction. The present volume is full of such thought-provoking ideas.

It also deals with the differences between prose in

general and the kind of prose which is sometimes called poetry. In this instance he discusses the application of the proper terms to Melville's Benito Cereno.

Some of the most compelling discussions appear in the chapter called "Fivf," the author's term for a "superclass" which helps us to distinguish between "fiction by value" and "fiction by intention." He expands the definition by analysis and example. Indeed, throughout this volume the author is notably concrete, not merely introducing ideas that he treats vaguely. He is modest in his approaches, but firm in making his points. This is, altogether, a useful and challenging book of criticism.

HARRY T. MOORE

Southern Illinois University
April 23, 1972

Introduction

This book began as a nagging dissatisfaction with the explanations of fiction I found in literary glossaries. I wanted to understand some very simple matters a little better than I did: how a collection of letters by Chesterfield was different from an epistolary novel by Smollett, say, and what a novel by Franz Kafka had in common with those Sue Barton stories my sisters used to read. I could see as well as anyone else when one book was fiction and when another was not, but I found it exasperatingly difficult to explain even to myself what the differences between them were. I was soon led into elaborately tortured distinctions among fictions, nonfictions, and frauds, and these eventually resolved into the theories I outline in the second and in the final chapters of this book.

However, the closer I came to finding a satisfactory answer to these questions, the more interested I became in the term *fiction* itself—or, more accurately, in the odd concept-structure to which it is presently attached. The critics themselves rarely suggest this in their definitions, but they are using this word—with absolute assurance—in what at first seems a hopeless tangle of different ways. Slowly I began to make sense of that tangle, and as I did I found I was beginning to see a logic behind literary criticism I had missed before. And so this book started as an irritation, developed into a theory of fiction, and finally transformed itself into something much more pretentious: a theory of the mind of the critic and of the laws that govern it.

It is a very common practice for teachers of linguistics to begin by asking their students to invent some new words. This the students do with no effort at all, and they end with lists that include *glud* and *roog* and *grinjfloos* and *melpfliz* and so forth. And then their teachers show them they have all been following—quite unconsciously —very, very complicated rules they have never heard of before, rules that determine precisely which kinds of syllables they can imagine and which they cannot: e.g., that they will not imagine a syllable that begins with the last sound in the word *sing,* for instance, or begin a syllable with an *ft.*[1] And from this the students gain two lessons. They learn that there are laws governing their verbal behavior hidden inside them; they learn that when they were very young they inferred rules of behavior which are so complicated they have the greatest difficulty understanding them consciously and yet that since childhood they have been following them unconsciously without the slightest effort. And the second lesson comes when they see that mere awareness there *are* such rules inside them is enough to free them from those rules; their subsequent word-lists include such barbarities as *ngkpsa* and *ftyl* and *dtrtas* in happy abundance. And this is the more important lesson, being one homely proof of the ancient wisdom that there is a kind of freedom that can be won merely through self-knowledge.

There are many reasons I give myself to justify the work required to design the theories I am presenting. In my most private moments I remind myself that it gives me the kinds of pleasure other people get from skiing and from writing poetry and from gardening. When someone I respect has just given me the ho-hums about one of my inventions, I nervously remind myself that theorizing about literary matters has a well-established tradition behind it and does not need justification anyhow. And I also have a "dirty little secret": I would like to win fame and fortune and be solemnly interviewed on the important questions of our time. But, really, I feel most comfortable when I can remind people of self-illuminations they won through linguistics or psychology or sociology or history and of the intellectual enlargements that sometimes followed. I hope that this book will do something like that for the literary critics who read it.

I want to acknowledge the help given in 1967 by a University of Connecticut Faculty Summer Fellowship, which freed me from teaching so that I might work on the materials I am presenting. I want to express my appreciation, also, to Dean Hugh Clark and to the Research Foundation for continuing aid and encouragement.

This does not end my indebtedness. This book was not dashed off at a single setting; it was worked up over many years of thought and discussion. The earliest versions of the theories presented here were in some cases only vaguely like those that finally emerged, and that is in part a result of discussions—often absurdly intense—I had with friends and with enemies. Especially helpful in one way or another were J. D. O'Hara, Bobbie Mason Rawlings, John Fraser, Roger Wilkenfeld, Charles McLaughlin, Jack Davis, Irving Cummings, Peter Thorslev, Arthur Wills, Edward Groff, Thomas Much, and Thomas Wilcox. Some of them will note with grim satisfaction that theories I was propounding a few years ago do not appear; their disagreements had that much effect on me, at least. The footnotes will indicate other debts I owe. I have provided a Bibliographical Note for the reader who would like to begin exploring these areas for himself.

THOMAS   J.   ROBERTS

Storrs, Connecticut
February 1972

When Is Something Fiction?

1

Some Essential Distinctions

The word *fiction* is not yet the single most important term in modern literary criticism, but it is certainly one of that very small group of terms now carrying the heaviest burdens in critical discourse. The words *fiction* and *poetry* and *drama* and *art* and *literature* are used in such a bewildering variety of ways that only the very plainest sentences employing them ever make clear sense to us. And I suspect that the word fiction is becoming increasingly more important: just as the word literature seems to have replaced the word poetry as the most general term in criticism, now the word fiction seems to be replacing it.

How are we using that word? We all think we know pretty well what it means, but we are not prepared to explain it in very precise detail. After only a little inquiry we impatiently conclude that the word is too vague to be exactly defined. Actually, the word is neither simple nor vague: it is immensely complex. It is we who are vague when we try to explain it.

I think the following theory will account for our usage of the word in contemporary criticism—that is, for all except very special and freakish uses. But the theory is itself very complex—as befits the phenomenon it explains—and I shall begin with a simple overview. After the major features of the theory are made plain I shall give detailed reconsideration of that general picture. Much of what I say at first may not be clear or convincing—because it is very compact and rests upon explanations to be given later—but I think the going does get easier very quickly. One other matter: the order in which I explain the various features of fiction's meaning is neither the order in which I discovered them (I shudder even to think of retracing that tangled path) nor the order in which it would most efficiently be presented in an argumentative situation, but rather the order which permits quickest comprehension.

Let us begin, then, by observing that the word fiction is now being given two radically dissimilar extensions: sometimes it is used to refer to a class of texts (including, say, Joyce's *Finnegans Wake* and Milton's *Paradise Lost* and Hawthorne's "Young Goodman Brown") but sometimes it is used to refer to a genre rather than to the specific books in that genre. Thus the word fiction is sometimes thought to refer to certain writing traditions —those of the novel of manners and the adventure story and the love lyric, for instance—rather than to certain books. Call that first usage *fiction as texts* and the second *fiction as genres*. It proves immensely difficult to handle them both at the same time, and so I will set the second of them aside for a long while. I will treat fiction as though it were only a question of texts for most of the first part of this essay; but I shall never be unaware that fiction is also a matter of genres, and I shall eventually be turning back to that notion and show how it is related to everything which has come before.

So now I am concerned only with the use of the word fiction to designate a particular class of texts. There are several different classes of texts that we shall have to be identifying, but all of them fit within one or another of two major classes. This, then, is the second major distinction we must recognize.

These two major classes intersect but are different. When I say the classes are different I mean merely that the criteria that earn a text membership in the one are different from those that earn a text membership in the other. When I say they intersect I mean nothing more than that there are some texts which are members of both classes—which meet both sets of criteria. Thus I am both a male human being and an American, but the fact that I belong to one of those classes does not guarantee I belong to the other: as it happens those two classes intersect at the class *male American human beings*.

There is, then, a superclass composed of two intersecting smaller classes. I give this superclass the name *fifv*: I will explain that name in just a moment. (A glossary at the back explains how this and other terms are used in this book, but it will not be very meaningful until after the reader has studied the explanations given in the text.) Think of that superclass as looking like a very plain capital *T*: two very simple rectangles overlapping, one vertical, one horizontal. One of the classes is the crossbar and the other the vertical stroke and they intersect where they cross.

This **T**-shaped superclass fifv is of fundamental importance. All texts are either inside fifv or outside it. If a text is not within the boundaries of fifv, no critic will ever call it fiction. The fact that a text is within fifv's boundaries does not guarantee any critic will name it fiction, but he will never name it fiction if it is not a part of fifv. And so if we have not yet identified either fiction or not-fiction we have managed to identify something we might call *never-fiction*: it is everything in the area outside fifv.

From this it will be clear that however slippery the word fiction proves to be we know it is always confined within the limits of fifv. But this does not imply that the word fiction means the same thing the word fifv means. It does not. No literary critic ever uses the word fiction to refer at any one moment to all of the area covered by fifv, and so we still have the meanings of fiction to seek.

Call these two different but intersecting classes in fifv by the following names: *fiction by intention* and *fiction by value*. (The name fifv can now be seen to be an acronym formed from the initial letters in these last two names.) Most books belong to neither of these two classes (they are outside fifv), but some books belong to one and some books belong to the other and a few books belong to both.

The first class—fiction by intention—includes all books written with a certain purpose. Roughly speaking, if a writer wanted his book to be taken by his readers as intentionally untrue in its facts, then it is an instance of fiction by intention.

More precisely: *A book is fiction by intention if its writer has knowingly made it factually untrue but also warned his readers he has done this.*

This definition could not stand without further explanation and qualification, for the distinctions the critic makes among such terms as fiction and lying and allegory and ironic quotation are many and tortured. Let us simply note here that all novels and short stories and passionate addresses to nonexistent Chloes and Amaryllises are fiction by intention and that much else is besides.

The other class—fiction by value—is far too mysterious to get any more than the very simplest and most evasive definition:

A book is fiction by value if it deserves to be deeply admired.

When I told a friend in a letter that I was puzzling out the meanings of the word fiction he expressed some sympathy but said that he had always felt fiction was merely "that which unlocks the frozen sea within." Clearly, he was not at that moment using the word with exclusive reference to novels and short stories; and in fact there is increasing evidence that while most literary critics give verbal definitions of the word fiction that point toward fiction by intention they blithely use the word often as a synonym or part-synonym for the words literature and poetry also. They are more ready to admit that the historical writings of Edward Gibbon are fiction than that current best-seller novels are—and that is to give the word a fiction-by-value orientation.

Our **T**-shaped superclass fifv has as its two major components fiction by intention and fiction by value. But each of these is further divided, and some subclasses in the one are subclasses in the other as well. This last fact is of fundamental importance also. The subclasses which are members of both major classes serve as a pivot on which the word fiction is made to shift in meaning— and with so little effort that the critic who is using the word is usually not even aware this is happening.

Consider a class of books we can call *great novels*. Let us have it include Tolstoy's *War and Peace* and Joyce's *Ulysses* and Austen's *Emma* and Eliot's *Middlemarch* and Dostoevsky's *Crime and Punishment*: critics are agreed they are novels and that if any books deserve to be called great they do. Let us have the group include the best short stories, too: Faulkner's "A Rose for Emily" and Crane's "The Open Boat" and Joyce's "The Dead" and so forth. (Sometimes critics like to distinguish between the novel and the romance, but let us have the great romances in this class too: Hawthorne's *Scarlet Letter* and Melville's *Moby-Dick* and others.) This group of books does constitute a discrete entity in the perceptions and speech of literary critics. And if we wanted to stop to reason it all out it would quickly become evident that this small class is fiction by intention by virtue of its members' being novels and romances and short stories and that it is also fiction by value by virtue of their being immensely valuable to critics.

As it happens, this small class—great novels—is one of several subclasses which are members of both the major components of fifv; but it is the most central of these several subclasses, and it is of the greatest importance to us. Whenever critics use the word fiction they are referring to great novels. More often than not, they are referring to something else in fifv as well, but they are always referring to this too. Call this the core meaning of the word fiction: it is also the pivot meaning.

The word fiction pivots on the meaning 'great novels.' It is not the only word in the critical vocabulary that operates in this way, we discover. The term poetry also pivots—on the meaning 'great lyrics'—between two major classes of texts, and apparently other words like drama and literature and serious writing pivot in this way too. It is a feature of critical discourse that has not been sufficiently remarked, and I shall be going into it more deeply later.

The minimum meaning of the word fiction is 'great novels.' The ultimate limits of the word's various meanings is fifv. But having learned only this we have not learned very much about the word's many extensions and we have learned almost nothing about the dynamics of critical activity. Let us shift our emphasis. At the moment we have a static view of the word fiction as having certain (as yet unspecified) meanings. If we visualize fifv as two rectangles overlapping to form a simple capital T, then we can add a small square within the area of overlap and think of that as the class of all great novels—that core meaning I have just been speaking of. Now let us add some directions for the employment of the word fiction with reference to that diagram. We will specify two rules we can already see are needed:

RULE A: *Always so use the word fiction that all the texts it refers to are within the class fifv.*

RULE B: *Always have the word fiction refer to at least the class of all great novels, whether it refers to anything else or not.*

And to this I can add a third rule which my observations suggest is needed:

RULE C: *When using the word fiction always observe either a fiction-by-intention orientation or a fiction-by-value orientation.*

A man who follows these rules will be approximating —very crudely—the customs of critics who use the word fiction. And we can increase the sophistication of his usage by identifying additional references and specifying additional rules for his guidance.

In the sections that follow I shall examine fiction by intention very closely and then turn to fiction by value. After I have identified the outer boundaries of these two major classes I shall specify their many interrelated subdivisions. We will then have a complete model of fifv which will serve to identify the divisions critics sense when they think of fiction as texts, and I shall return to the concept of fiction as genres and show that it exists as a kind of antimatter universe precisely paralleling that of fiction as texts. It will then be possible to give a fuller rules-specification for the uses of the word fiction and to suggest some of the implications of the theory.

2

Fiction by Intention

Consider the following two lists. A little study will show that the books in the first group display a curious kind of invention which is related to lying but is not quite that and that those in the second group do not have this one kind of invention.

1. Tolstoy's *Anna Karenina*, Twain's *Huckleberry Finn*, *Sir Gawain and the Green Knight*, Metalious's *Peyton Place*, Susann's *Valley of the Dolls*, Mitchell's *Gone With the Wind*, Coleridge's "Rime of the Ancient Mariner," Frost's "The Witch of Coös," Service's "Shooting of Dan McGrew," Noyes's "Highwayman," Addison and Steele's *Sir Roger de Coverley Papers*, Dunne's *Mr. Dooley's Philosophy*, Holmes's "Autocrat of the Breakfast Table," Goldsmith's *She Stoops to Conquer*, Shakespeare's *Twelfth Night*.

2. Boswell's *Life of Johnson*, Gibbon's *Decline and Fall of the Roman Empire*, Burton's *Anatomy of Melancholy*, Carlyle's *Sartor Resartus*, Darwin's *Origin of Species*, Milton's *Paradise Lost*, Lucretius's *De rerum natura*, Dante's *Divine Comedy*, Edwards's *Freedom of the Will*, Pope's *Essay on Man*, Hemans's "Landing of the Pilgrim Fathers," Thackeray's "Pocahontas," Halleck's "Marco Bozzaris," *The 1967 Sears-Roebuck Catalog*, and *The Cambridge Bibliography of English Literature*.

I designed these lists myself, of course, but the distinctions they suggest are genuinely important to critics. The works in the first group are fiction by intention; those in the second are not. But what is it the books in the first group have that makes them fiction by intention?

Let us first approach the question negatively. Certain very important critical distinctions are *not* involved in determining whether something is or is not fiction by intention. The distinctions between prose and verse, for instance: I put prose works in both lists (*Anna Karenina* in the first, for instance, and *The Life of Johnson* in the second) and also examples of verse (e.g., "Rime of the Ancient Mariner" and *Paradise Lost*). Nor is the distinction between the admirable and the not-admirable involved—whatever that might be. I was careful to include in each list works critics agree are admirable (the works of Tolstoy and Twain and Coleridge, for instance, and those of Boswell and Burton and Dante) and a selection of others they agree are not admirable: the works listed for Metalious, Susann, Service, Noyes, Hemans, Thackeray, and Halleck. And a distinction which will be important to us later is not important to us here: the distinction between works having a narrative element and those which do not: *Anna Karenina* and *Paradise Lost* have narrative elements in them but neither the Holmes essay in the first group has nor does the Sears-Roebuck catalog in the second. Nor do differences in length or in date of publication or in language of composition enter the matter.

Some of these differences are important when we identify various subsections within fiction by intention, but we are not concerned about that right now. Once again: *A book is fiction by intention if its writer has knowingly made it factually untrue but also warned his readers he has done this*. All of the works in the first list meet these conditions, but none of those in the second list do.

Here is a closely similar definition anthropologists have turned up:

> "We do not really mean, we do not really mean, that what we are going to say is true" is the traditional beginning of every Ashanti tale. The Sudanese regard their tales as lies in which not everything is false—lies containing a grain of truth, a form of wisdom, common sense, and a moral. Storytelling sessions usually begin with the following formula:
>
> > "I'm going to tell a story," the narrator begins.
> > "Right!" the audience rejoins.
> > "It's a lie."
> > "Right!"
> > "But not everything in it is false."
> > "Right!"
>
> It ends with the formula: "I put the tale back where I found it." [1]

When we compare this ritual beginning with the definition that preceded it we discover that the Sudanese are conscious of very much the same distinctions that interest the American literary critic. The Sudanese work with fiction by intention too.

We need that definition of ours if we want to make explicit that intricate set of distinctions critics make unconsciously when they decide that *Anna Karenina* and *Twelfth Night* are significantly like one another (and like all the other books in my first list) but significantly unlike such works as *The Life of Johnson* and *De rerum natura*. And they do make that distinction. They may not use the phrase fiction by intention: this is one of the many occasions on which they would speak of the distinction between fiction and nonfiction. But they see those many works as like one another, and that is a perception of the class we shall be calling, less ambiguously, fiction by intention. And now we must look at that definition more closely. If it is to survive the test of daily use it will need much explanation and also some qualification.

The concept of the fact, of factuality, of what has been called "realistic particularity,"[2] is crucial to the definition. Critics do recognize a distinction between the general and the factual, and the distinction is important to them: "There is factual truth, truth in specific detail of time and place—truth of history in the narrow sense. Then there is philosophic truth: conceptual, propositional, general."[3] But it is important that we dissociate the concept of truth from the concepts of generality and factuality. Tolstoy's *Anna Karenina* begins: "Happy families are all alike; every unhappy family is unhappy in its own way." Perhaps this is true, perhaps it is not. True or untrue, the sentence is not factual but general, or propositional. Nathaniel Hawthorne's short story, "The Birthmark," has the following sentences: "In the centre of Georgiana's left cheek there was a singular mark, deeply interwoven, as it were, with the texture and substance of her face. In the usual state of her complexion—a healthy though delicate bloom—the mark wore a tint of deeper crimson, which imperfectly defined its shape amid the surrounding rosiness. . . . Its shape bore not a little similarity to the human hand, though of the smallest pygmy size." From the writer's point of view, at least, these sentences were not true: the Georgiana referred to did not exist. But the sentences are factual. Fiction deals in untrue specificities, untrue facts. The books written by Henry Adams and Edward Gibbon and Herodotus and Charles Darwin and those written by Henry James and J. R. R. Tolkien and William Faulkner include statements critics recognize as factual: they make reference to specific details of time and place. But Kant's *Critique of Pure Reason* and Spinoza's *Ethics* do not include the kind of statement critics call factual. The distinctions critics recognize do not seem to be very sophisticated, but they do recognize distinctions. A page torn from a telephone directory will seem only factual to critics, a philosophical monograph will seem only nonfactual, but novels and biographies will seem both general and factual.

Unless the text includes statements of fact, it will never seem to be fiction by intention to the critic. This is not to say that the wholly nonfactual text will not sometimes be called fiction. It will; because, as we have already seen, the word fiction sometimes extends outside the boundaries of fiction by intention. But we are not interested in the word fiction at the moment: we are only interested in identifying clearly the boundaries of fiction by intention.

A work is not fiction by intention, to critics, unless the man who wrote it thought it was factually untrue. If he did not deliberately make it untrue in this way, at least he allowed that to happen and believes it is factually untrue. The distinction is small and it is easily missed, but it is essential. Is the text itself factually true? The question is unimportant. Did its writer think it factually untrue? That is the question the critic unconsciously asks himself. If we ask both these questions about any selection of factual texts we find that they divide those books into four simple groups: 1) those true books their writers know are true,   2) those false books their writers mistakenly think true,   3) those false books their writers know are false, and   4) those true books their writers mistakenly think false. All fiction by intention comes from the last of these two groups. Other kinds of books that are not fiction by intention are found in those two groups as well, but it is only there that fiction by intention is found.

Consider briefly the four classes we have discovered.

The first includes those books their writers correctly think are factually true. I can produce such a text by making a scrupulously accurate listing of the brute facts of my life for an entry in a biographical dictionary, say. To the best of our present knowledge, most of the history and science textbooks now being used fall into this category.

The second class is hard to keep distinct in one's mind from the last two and is constantly giving people who talk about fiction difficulty. These are the books written by sincere men who happen to have been mistaken. Seventeenth- and eighteenth-century accounts of scientific phenomena were often mistaken, but we do not classify them as fiction by intention: their writers did not think them factually untrue. I suppose the original writer of Genesis may have thought he was giving a simple, accurate, factual account of the creation of the universe, but we do not agree with him. And we do not recognize his work as fiction by intention. It is not the presence or absence of factual credibility in a text that interests the critic: if a piece of primitive history has whales speaking to men but it is quite evident that the peoples who pass on that story believe it to be factually true, the critic may find it charming in the way some fiction by intention is charming; but he will identify it as mistaken history, not fiction by intention.[4]

That leaves us with two groups of books. The writers of both groups were convinced the books were factually unture. In one case they are right, in the other they are wrong. The immense bulk of fiction by intention is comprised of books whose authors knowingly made them factually untrue. When Henry James wrote the story of *The Ambassadors* he knew that the events he narrated were not literally true. This is not to say that this novel does not contain philosophic truth, or that James was lying to his readers, or even that some of the events did not occur, or that *some* of his descriptions are not factually true. But it is the case that the story in *The Ambassadors* is not literally true in the sense that the story in Boswell's *Life of Johnson* is literally true. And it is the case that, say, the seventeenth-century writer who gave an account of the theory of humours which we now feel is literally untrue was different from Henry James, who also gave a literally untrue account, in that the former did not recognize the events he described never took place. The critic says the seventeenth-century physician wrote mistaken medicine but that Henry James—knowingly and openly creating factual untruths—was writing fiction by intention.

Most fiction by intention is in this one of the four groups of books I distinguished: those books of which it can be said both that they are factually untrue and that their authors knew that. But fiction by intention is not confined to that one group, for the author's intention [5] is always more important to the critic than the book's factual truth. A text may be literally true and still be regarded as fiction by intention if it is certain its author thought it was not literally true. Let us give some consideration to this awkward class of books because much confusion about fiction by intention arises if we do not have that class clearly understood.

Just as it is perfectly possible for any man to tell what he thinks is the truth and be mistaken, so it is possible for a man to tell what he thinks is an untruth and be mistaken. Many a novelist has discovered that though he invented a grotesque name for one of his characters and gave him an exotic residence and quite improbable features—all in the attempt to avoid seeming to be talking about any real person—this did not save him from a court judgment of damages against him when a living person with that name and residence and some of those improbable features sued for the payment of damages done him by that novel. The courts have held that the books were factually true to the plaintiff in at least enough respects to make readers feel the plaintiff was the referent of the text—even though the courts also knew that the novelist had not intended to refer to the plaintiff. Here is a moderately typical instance:

> A certain publicity campaign for the *Topper* movie series put on by the Hal Roach studios in the 1940's involved sending out torrid letters on scented pink stationery to several hundred men selected at random; they were signed "Marion Kerby," the name of the female ghost in the movies and in the original story by Thorne Smith. It happened that there lived in the Los Angeles area a woman named Marion Kerby, who sued the studio on the ground that her privacy had been invaded and her reputation damaged; and . . . she won her case when "the judge held that the letters did refer to her in a clear and definite fashion." [6]

Texts such as these are literally true even though it was not intended that they be. Because the author did not intend them to be true—in spite of the fact that they are true—the critic continues to feel they are fiction by intention.

But, now, having said this, it is necessary to make a large qualification. It is possible—more, it is likely—that a writer of fiction by intention will regard most of the factual statements in his novel, say, as true. Even when this is the case, the critic will accept that book as fiction by intention if certain other conditions obtain.

A thing—a book, say, or a sentence—is made fiction by intention by being handed to someone else in a certain way. Any sentences anyone could devise are acceptable to a critic as fiction by intention if they appear within the right kind of context: even now, the very propositions that in one book are accepted as historical are accepted in another as fiction by intention. The same sentences a novelist will write into his journal as a description of London may later appear in his novels: in the novels they are fiction by intention, in the journal they are not. For any author at any time there are always some sentences he could not write without feeling them factually true and others he could not write without feeling them factually untrue: most of that author's books will include a selection of both kinds of sentences and the critic will recognize that and still insist that though the author's opinion of their truth overrides all the considerations the book is fiction by intention.

It is a question of the structural relationship between those sentences the writer thought factually false and those he thought factually true. Typically, a work of fiction by intention is a small or large body of propositions the author thinks true—even in many cases factually true—framed by a small or large body of propositions the author thinks false. If the critic feels that the framing sentences in the book were regarded by the writer as factually untrue (and the book meets certain other conditions we have yet to explore), then he will accept the whole book as fiction by intention.

In many cases, the differences between the framing and the framed portions are quite plain: the frame appears in different sentences from those in which the framed appears. The novel tells us that a man named Ahab speaks, or a Tom Jones, or a Chillingsworth. The sentences that tell us that constitute part of the fiction-by-intention frame; we know the writer recognizes that those sentences are not literally true. When a fiction-by-intention character speaks, the critic simply categorizes anything he says as fiction by intention also. A Leopold Bloom or a Rhett Butler or a Hamlet may quote from the Bible, he may give information his author has plagiarized from a statistical handbook, he may give a lovingly detailed and accurate description of the room in which the writer is then sitting, he may utter a prayer that some devout reader adopts to his own purposes later; whatever it is that fiction-by-intention creation says is accepted as itself fiction by intention.

This is not a unique feature of the twentieth-century reader. It is plainly evident in earlier readers. Here Sir Philip Sidney in his *Apology for Poetry* argues that Plato's dialogues are examples of what he called poetry but we are calling fiction by intention:

> For all standeth upon dialogues, wherein he feigneth many honest burgesses of Athens to speak of such matters, that, if they had been set on the rack, they would never have confessed them, besides his poetical describing the circumstances of their meetings, as the well ordering of a banquet, the delicacy of a walk, with interlacing mere tales, as Gyges' Ring, and others, which who knoweth not to be flowers of poetry did never walk into Apollo's garden.

If critics were pedantically committed to the belief that anything framed by fiction-by-intention sentences is fiction by intention, we might create instances enough with a very trivial strategy: we would write "Mercutio said," at the beginning of any book—a Spanish dictionary, say, or Wittgenstein's *Philosophical Investigations*, or a history of Bulgaria—and we would have created something critics would feel obliged to call a novel. But of course they do not respond so mechanically. Most critics would prefer to say that Plato's *Dialogues* are philosophical essays with thin and unessential coatings of fiction by intention, and it is probably this attitude they have toward all those many dialogue-expositions they read: Oscar Wilde's exposition of his theories on the relations between art and nature in his *Decay of Lying* and Clara Reeve's distinctions between the novel and the romance in her *Progress of Romance* and John Dryden's *Essay of Dramatic Poesy,* and so forth.[7] And yet it must be said that a very slight skeleton of fiction-by-intention propositions will move a great mass of true sentences into the realm of fiction by intention.

Of course, the dialogue is not a very important instance of fiction by intention for the critic. He normally deals with books in which the fiction-by-intention frame is very difficult to separate from the other materials it carries. Take *Moby-Dick,* for instance.

> There are evidently two if not three books in Moby Dick rolled into one. Book No. 1 we could describe as a thorough exhaustive account admirably given of the great Sperm Whale. . . . Book No. 2 is the romance of Captain Ahab, Queequeg, Tashtego, Pip & Co., who are more or less spiritual personages talking and acting differently from the general business run of the conversation on the decks of whalers.[8]

Huge chunks of *Moby-Dick* are plainly fiction by intention; other huge chunks are plainly not—the descriptions of whaling procedures, most notably. But much of the book has fiction-by-intention propositions and other propositions combined in the same sentences. We make a purely mental separation of the two kinds—as we do in the case of all those other books we say are fiction by intention (e.g., novels) that nevertheless give a good impression of fifteenth-century Germany (i.e., Reade's *Cloister and the Hearth*) or of the personalities of working scientists (the novels of C. P. Snow) or of marriage relationships (Tolstoy's *Anna Karenina*) or of something we might also turn elsewhere to learn about.

And now let us put this qualification together with that earlier distinction between the thinks-true and the thinks-false. The definition of fiction by intention says that the writer must think his book factually untrue if the critic is to accept it as fiction by intention. It is not important whether the book be factually true or factually false: a factually false book is not thereby fiction by intention nor is a factually true book thereby eliminated from fiction by intention. It is wholly a question of the writer's feeling (rightly *or* wrongly) that his book is factually untrue. Further, the writer may include in his book propositions he feels are factually true—so long as they appear within a fiction-by-intention context, or frame—and still have his book accepted as fiction by intention.

What do I mean when I say a book is factually untrue? I say a book is factually untrue when the image it induces in my mind does not match in fact-for-fact fashion the image reality puts in my mind, and I suppose critics must operate in this way, too. We feel that the story of George Washington and the cherry tree is factually untrue: a book that repeats that story implants a certain conception in our minds when we read it, but reality (in this case, the other texts that give us our most trusted conception of that particular piece of reality) gives a conception which does not jibe fact-for-fact with Parson Weems's story. This is what we are saying when we say a book is factually untrue. We do not require that the text- and the reality-induced conceptions be factually identical; we expect the image reality induces in our brains to be much richer factually than the one a text will put there,[9] but we do require a certain asymmetrical one-for-one fact-correspondence: for every fact in the image we get from the text there must be a matching fact in the image we get from reality. When every text-fact has a matching reality-fact, then—even though there be many reality-facts left over—we declare the text to be literally true, to be factually true.

May a factually untrue book be propositionally true? This is as certain as it is that a factually true book may be propositionally untrue. Figures don't lie, but liars figure: this tedious saw asserts that we cannot trust the literally true to be propositionally true. By a careful selection and arrangement of the facts of your life I can make you seem either a demon or a hero. But it is also possible that I might invent literally untrue facts about you and through them convey an impression of you which was highly accurate. No doubt many a patriotic nineteenth-century American parent telling the story of George Washington and his cherry tree knew that it was factually untrue and yet felt that the story suggested something about Washington that truly was in the man. I suspect that almost everybody invents factually untrue accounts regularly without ever really thinking of them as lies. For most of us it is only a matter of modifying the known facts (we exaggerate a bit here and play down some other things there) in the interest of getting larger truths across; but I have often noticed quite moral friends wholly invent, or at least adapt, stories in order to make a point. If we know a man is brave or honest or deceitful or selfish, but we do not have a literally true story conveniently in mind, we sometimes invent a story—factually a lie, or factually true but out of some other person's life—and tell that in the interests of getting people to see that he is courageous or selfish or has whatever other quality it is we have seen in him. When religious people do this, they call these lies pious legends, but probably most of the rest of us have done this at one time or another and have hardly even noticed what it is we did. This is a very dangerous kind of thing to do, but it requires a very sophisticated morality to make one feel guilty about it: it is precisely because this liar wants his listeners to know and feel the truth that he engages in his act of factual deception.[10] If this is lying, and it is, it is also a moral kind of lying.

When a writer invents facts in order to give a true general impression of something—of life or love or whaling or the loss of innocence—and then tells us he has invented those facts, we have one kind of fiction by intention: a truth-telling fiction by intention.

A book may be fiction by intention if its writer has knowingly made it factually untrue—but only if he warns his readers he has done this. This distinction, too, is essential. If I tell someone something I know is factually untrue but I do not warn him of this, I am lying to him. This is only one kind of lie (lies are more complicated and various than fiction by intention), but it is the commonest and it is precisely the one that the simple-minded have most often confused with fiction by intention. Fiction is lies, they tell us, because the writer is knowingly telling untruths.

How are factual lies different from fiction by intention? The first difference that occurs to us is that the liar is trying to deceive us and the writer of fiction by intention is not. But the distinction is subtler than that. Much fiction by intention was intended to deceive us. What else are we to say of a book that begins with the following sentences?

I had this story from one who had no business to tell it to me, or to any other. I may credit the seductive influence of an old vintage upon the narrator for the beginning of it, and my own skeptical incredulity during the days that followed for the balance of the strange tale.

When my convivial host discovered that he had told me so much, and that I was prone to doubtfulness, his foolish pride assumed the task the old vintage had commenced, and so he unearthed written evidence in the form of musty manuscript, and dry official records of the British Colonial Office to support many of the salient features of his remarkable narrative.

I do not say the story is true, for I did not witness

the happenings which it portrays, but the fact that in
the telling of it to you I have taken fictitious names
for the principal characters quite sufficiently evidences
the sincerity of my own belief that it *may* be true.

These are the opening paragraphs of *Tarzan of the
Apes*.[11] And Sax Rohmer's *The Insidious Dr. Fu Manchu*
is prefaced with the following disclaimer:

This book is fiction. No resemblance is intended between any character herein and any person, living or
dead; any such resemblance is purely coincidental.

But by the time we have reached chapter 24, we find we
are reading sentences which say quite the opposite.

From the rescue of Lord Southery my story bears me
mercilessly on to other things. I may not tarry, as more
leisurely penmen, to round out my incidents; they
were not of my choosing. I may not pause to make
you better acquainted with the figure of my drama;
its scheme is none of mine.

Anyone who browses through a collection of the observations of novelists on novel-writing will quickly
become convinced that for many of them the problem
of finding a way to deceive their readers into accepting
the facts as true has been of central concern.

The real, if unavowed, purpose of fiction is to give
pleasure by gratifying the love of the uncommon in
human experience, mental or corporeal.
    This is done all the more perfectly in proportion as
the reader is illuded to believe the personages true and
real like himself.

This was Thomas Hardy speaking,[12] and here is Ford
Maddox Ford: "The object of the novelist is to keep the

reader entirely oblivious of the fact that the author exists—even of the fact that he is reading a book." [13]

All liars are trying to deceive us, but many writers of fiction by intention are trying to deceive us too. Clearly, it is not the attempt to deceive that makes the difference for critics between the factual lie and fiction by intention. Nor, of course, is the distinction between the two a matter of the one having honorable and the other having only base motives; or of, say, fiction-by-intention's having desirable and lies' having disagreeable results. Many of our lies have honorable motives and desirable results: as when the physician assures his patient he is healthy because he knows any other news would drive the man into an insanity of despair. And writers of fiction by intention sometimes do it only to earn money or to make themselves well known.

A writer may do everything in his power to deceive us into accepting his book as wholly true, but if he gives us fair warning that it is not factually true, then we say he is writing fiction by intention and not lies. The simple-minded enemies of fiction by intention were right in saying the writer of fiction by intention is knowingly telling untruths and they were right in saying he is (often) trying to deceive us. They were wrong to brush hastily over those signals the writer gives to alert his readers that his book should be taken as neither factually a lie nor as factually a mistake but as something different from either.

What persuades the critics that the writer wanted his readers to be alerted? Some prefatory statement. Here is Lucian introducing his *True History* with about as clear a warning as one is ever likely to find:

> I am telling you frankly, here and now, that I have no intention whatever of telling the truth. Let this voluntary confession forestall any future criticism: I

am writing about things entirely outside my own experience or anyone else's, things that have no reality whatever and never could have. So mind you do not believe a word I say.[14]

Or certain kinds of labels attached to the title of the work. If the writer had attached the word *Novel,* or *Romance,* or *Tale,* or *Entertainment,* or *Fantasia,* or some synonym of one of these, the critic will accept that, of course, as ample evidence that the writer was openly presenting what he thought was a factually untrue text as just that.[15] If the writer then proceeded to use every device at his command to make the reader *forget* the warning he had been given, this does not affect the text's status for the critics as fiction by intention.

Of course, things are a bit more complicated and interesting than that. Many—perhaps most—texts accepted as fiction by intention have no such label; but in these cases, certain other things are taken as indications of an authorial intention that the reader be forewarned. Perhaps contemporary accounts make it clear the writer expected the text to be printed in a journal which would list it in the table of contents under some such label as *Fiction,* or perhaps he knew that readers had come to expect all his work to be fiction by intention.

Further, if the text includes certain kinds of materials —a report of a conversation between secluded people just before they die (a conversation no living human being could have heard), or an interior monologue, or if it is a recent text but ascribes fantastic powers to people (the ability to read minds or to become invisible)—then we will feel that we had had sufficient warning and that the author could be expected to withhold those labels. We believe that no writer would be so foolish as to imagine either that his readers would think such material biography or journalism or history, or that they would think he was trying to deceive them into accepting it as biography or journalism. Such materials may be said to be stylistic indicators to the reader that the text is fiction by intention, and the text that includes such materials is not required to have warnings attached. Though it would be a waste of energy, I think, to search among purely stylistic features in the hopes of finding there the distinctive features of fiction by intention, stylistic indicators of this kind are important in their own way.[16]

In such cases, the critic would not claim that an authorial forewarning had been given but can very well reply to whatever innocent should accuse the writer of lying that the author would have thought such a warning redundant. The definition of fiction by intention we are examining declares that the writer of the book must have warned his readers that he has knowingly made it factually untrue: more accurately—but more clumsily—it would say that the writer *wanted* his readers to be forewarned.

But a curious exception to this rule must be recognized, too. If I write a factually untrue book and do not warn my readers it is factually untrue, literary critics will not accept that book as fiction by intention. This seems plain enough: it explains why it is that critics do not regard the stories printed in the American magazines *True Story* and *True Confessions* as fiction by intention and why they feel a book like "Jan Valtin's" *Out of the Night* (tactfully characterized later as "a highly unreliable autobiography," it attracted much attention just before the Second World War) is not fiction by intention.

But there are some intriguing exceptions to this rule. Daniel Defoe's *Robinson Crusoe* and *Moll Flanders*, for instance, and Mrs. Aphra Behn's *Oroonoko* were taken by their authors to be factually untrue but were not accompanied by a warning to the reader—yet the literary critics insist upon calling them novels and fiction. This is very curious behavior; it is not consistent with other identifications literary critics make. A variety of reasons can be offered to explain why critics identify Defoe's books as fiction, but the two most important reasons would seem to be these. First, these books are regarded by literary critics as admirable, and (as we shall see) any book critics think admirable is likely to be named fiction. Second, these books have been passed on from one generation of readers to the next with clear editorial—though not authorial—warnings of their factual untruth attached to them. This second matter is of some interest. Apparently, a shift in status from that of the lie to that of fiction by intention may be effected by later editors. No critic today picks up *Moll Flanders* without knowing beforehand it is not literally true, and even though it is Defoe's editors who are warning him and not Defoe himself, the book will still seem very closely similar to those works which have authorial warnings attached.[17]

My last qualification of that definition has fewer practical consequences than those I have already offered. It is this: that the critic will not think a text fiction by intention even if it does meet all the conditions outlined so far unless its writer also thought the text had some merit. This qualification becomes necessary if we try to distinguish between fiction by intention and ironic quotation. The need for distinguishing between the two rarely—perhaps never—arises for a literary critic, and so it is not very important practically. Still, let us look very briefly at the distinction.

Suppose I were to write a paraphrase of a description some earlier scholar had given of the life of Christopher Marlowe—a description that was wholly mistaken in its facts—and suppose, further, that I were to give that paraphrase as a preliminary to my own refutation of that description: scholars are doing this sort of thing all the

time, of course, and when they do that they are producing texts which, as it happens, meet all the conditions in
the definition of fiction by intention. And yet I do not
think any critic would feel about that paraphrase just the
way he would feel about, say, a retelling (in the same
number of words—the length of the text is not important) of that story of Washington and the cherry tree if
the retelling were preceded by the remark that the story
was silly but still naïvely charming.

I conclude—somewhat hesitantly—that there must be
something positive in the writer's presentation of a
factual text he feels is untrue: he must feel the text has
some merit beyond that of serving as a point of departure
for his own more accurate account. If he does not, the
critic will not feel the text is fiction by intention.

One might construct a definition of fiction by intention which makes explicit all these necessary explanations
and qualifications. It would look something like this:

Critics identify a text as fiction by intention when
they are persuaded that a) it is factual in some respects,
b) its writer thought all of it factually untrue or
thought, at least, that a particular set of factual propositions which frames all other propositions in the book
was untrue, c) he took the trouble to warn his readers
of this (or had reason to believe they would assume that
anyway) or his later editors warned them of that, and
d) he thought his text was valuable in some way even if
it was factually untrue.

This is reasonably accurate, but it is torturous to the
point of near-unintelligibility. Elegance has its uses, too.
Let us say, less clearly but more intelligibly, that *a book
is fiction by intention if its writer has knowingly made it
factually untrue but also warns his readers he has done
this*. But let us understand this second, simpler definition to mean everything the longer definition means.

This is fiction by intention, which is one major division

within fifv. Before proceeding to fiction by value, which is the other major division, I am going to conduct an experiment with fiction by intention. I want to show, first, that no sentence is intrinsically fiction by intention and, second, that a simple identification of any text as fiction by intention has profound consequences in critical attitudes. I shall take two sentences and force them to move from one side of the boundaries of fiction by intention to the other, and I shall comment on some of the effects this has upon us as readers.[18]

I have taken the following two sentences verbatim from *An Encyclopedia of World History*, revised edition, compiled and edited by William L. Langer, (Boston: Houghton, 1948).

> Xerxes, who had succeeded Darius in 486, demanded earth and water (submission) from all the Greek states, most of which refused. Xerxes thereupon led a carefully prepared expedition of about 180,000 men (not the traditional 900,000) into Greece through Thrace and Macedonia. (P. 54)

We will all agree that these two sentences are not fiction by intention as they appear in the *Encyclopedia of World History*. (We would normally say they were nonfiction, but the word *nonfiction* offers as many problems as the word fiction and I shall avoid it as much as I can.) We feel the writer believes these sentences are factually true and that he wants us to believe that too. We will be disappointed in those sentences if we feel they are *not* factually true.

But now let us suppose someone writes a novel into which he copies these two sentences. We need not suppose it is a good novel, just that it is a novel—a narrative piece of fiction by intention in prose. To make things easy for us, let us suppose that the novel purports to describe the life Shakespeare's Prospero and Miranda lived on that island before they were discovered in *The Tempest*. (And now *I* am creating a piece of fiction by intention about another piece of fiction by intention, but let us just ignore that whole tangle.) In the novel, the wizard Prospero is telling his daughter about the Greeks and their victories in the Persian wars.

"And now," Prospero said, "it is time for us to return to the history of Greece.

"Xerxes, who had succeeded Darius in 486, demanded earth and water (submission) from all the Greek states, most of which refused. Xerxes thereupon led a carefully prepared expedition of about 180,000 men (not the traditional 900,000) into Greece through Thrace and Macedonia."

"And did the Persians conquer the Greeks?" asked Miranda.

We have taken sentences which were not fiction by intention when we found them and subordinated them to a fiction-by-intention frame. In doing this we have pushed those sentences into fiction by intention. When will we as critics feel disappointed in those sentences now?

Even if those sentences are factually true—and we think they are—they may still disappoint us in this new context. If, for instance, they do not seem to have any role to play in the novel, we would be disappointed in them. If those sentences are not factually true, then we feel they have no place in the *Encyclopedia of World History* in which I found them, but we might be quite pleased with them in the novel. If the sentences are untrue but they serve to advance that novel—through revealing something about Prospero we would not otherwise know or in preparing us for something that will happen later in the novel—then we will be quite pleased with them and probably be amused at anyone who fastened, in this case, on their factual untruth as an excuse for condemning the writer. And even if someone were to prove to us that the writer of that novel wanted to copy them out of the *Encyclopedia of World History* accurately but failed to do that, we might still be satisfied with them if they performed well in the novel's terms.

As I suggested earlier, a sentence may be fiction by intention even if the writer thought it factually true. Once we do identify it as fiction by intention we lose interest in its literal truthfulness. Those two sentences from the *Encyclopedia of World History* have been framed by fiction-by-intention sentences and thereby transformed into fiction by intention. Let us push those sentences out of fiction by intention once more—not by removing the frame but by putting another frame around that. It is easy enough to do this: we merely suppose that whole passage from the novel has been quoted in a book review.

This novel is very uneven. At times, the wit and insight of the author carries the reader gratefully along with him, but at other times it is simply flat. Here, for instance:

"And now," Prospero said, "it is time for us to return to the history of Greece.

"Xerxes, who had succeeded Darius in 486, demanded earth and water (submission) from all the Greek states, most of which refused. Xerxes thereupon led a carefully prepared expedition of about 180,000 men (not the traditional 900,000) into Greece through Thrace and Macedonia."

"And did the Persians conquer the Greeks?" asked Miranda.

We can find that sort of thing in any history, and I fail to understand why the writer insists his readers endure all of the education they are ready to imagine Miranda must have received.

Now the sentences—twice enframed—are once again outside the boundaries of fiction by intention. They have the same status that quotations in a literary history have: the sentences that are fiction by intention in Dickens's *Great Expectations* become something else when they are quoted in a book on his novels.

It is true that we can focus on just those two central sentences and think of them as belonging properly inside the *Encyclopedia of World History*; but if we think of them as only a subordinate part of that review, then they are something else. In this context they are no longer fiction by intention. But they are no longer what they were originally, either.

Let us ask that helpful question once again: When will we as critics be disappointed in these sentences as they appear in the book review? We will be disappointed in them if they are not factually true—but the correspondence we demand is not the one we demanded when we read them in the history book. When we read them in the *Encyclopedia of World History*, we required that the factual propositions they generated in our minds match in one-to-one fashion the factual propositions all documents relevant to the Persian wars generate in our minds. Now, however, we ask only that they match the sentences that appear in the novel that is being reviewed. So long as these sentences are literally true to the text of the novel they need not be literally true to the realities of ancient Greece: in this case, it is the novel which is the reality to which they refer.

This simple exercise is important to me because it indicates pretty clearly that no sentence can properly be said to be intrinsically fiction by intention, it highlights the importance of framing materials within any text, and it shows me that while my identifications of books as fiction by intention or as something else may be quite unconscious, those identifications are activating various dispositional sets in my mind. If my brain has decided a book is not fiction by intention, I find myself confronting it with one set of questions: I am concerned about its factual truth, for instance. But when my brain has decided the book *is* fiction by intention, many of those questions are blanked out and some quite new questions intrigue me; and even when I am asking the same questions I find that I have a different sense of their importance relative to one another: that question about the book's factual truth is now very, very low in order of priority, for instance.

I shall return to fiction by intention in the last chapter. It is a curious human invention, though it is so familiar to us now that we find it very difficult to imagine that anyone might not be fully at ease with it.

3

Fiction by Value

Fiction by value is the other major part of fifv, and it is probably a more important part of the critic's sense of the word fiction than is fiction by intention. But sometimes the tradition controlling the verbal definition of a term may lag behind the tradition controlling its deployment, and this has happened in the case of the word fiction. Our dictionaries and our glossaries of literary terminology direct us always toward fiction by intention in their explanations of that word, and yet the critic does not restrict himself in his deployment of the word fiction to this one area.

I used to set a question for students in my classes in literary theory which asked that they tell us what they would have to do to transform a biography into fiction. It seemed to me a moderately good question: it made them think about their own thought-patterns; it was a question they could not answer simply by paraphrasing some aesthetician; and it was not something too difficult for them to tackle. It proved to be a very difficult question indeed: I discovered quickly that they all took it for granted I was asking them to tell me the difference between literature and subliterature and that they felt they would have to make the biography a great book in order to make it fiction. And in spite of my protestations in later attempts to use the question, they continued to feel that the difference between fiction and not-fiction is a difference between greatness and triviality. And they have learned this from their teachers and from the critics they have read. It is not the way I had been using the word, but it is as valid as any other, and we must look at it carefully.

I began my examination of fiction by intention with two lists of books. Here are some of the same titles, but they are now arranged differently. The books in the first list are in fiction by value, the books in the second are not.

1. Tolstoy's *Anna Karenina*, Mark Twain's *Huckle-berry Finn*, Coleridge's "Rime of the Ancient Mariner," Robert Frost's "The Witch of Coös," Holmes's "The Autocrat of the Breakfast Table," Boswell's *Life of Johnson*, Burton's *Anatomy of Melancholy*, Carlyle's *Sartor Resartus*, Milton's *Paradise Lost*, Dante's *Divine Comedy*, Lucretius's *De rerum natura*, Darwin's *Origin of Species*, Jonathan Edwards's *Freedom of the Will*, Locke's *An Essay Concerning Human Understanding*, Joshua Reynolds's *Discourses*, Kingslake's *Eothen*, Adam Smith's *Wealth of Nations*.

2. Metalious's *Peyton Place*, Susann's *Valley of the Dolls*, Service's "The Shooting of Dan McGrew," Noyes's "The Highwayman," Heman's "The Landing of the Pilgrim Fathers," Thackeray's "Pochahontas," Halleck's "Marco Bozzaris," *The 1967 Sears-Roebuck Catalog*.[1]

I would add Prescott's *Conquest of Mexico* to the first list, but I would put Spock's *Baby and Child Care* in the second. I would add the poems of Rod McKuen to the second list, the poems of Wallace Stevens to the first. It could not be made plain in lists as short as these; but the first is a list of books critics think great, and the second is a list of books critics think not of high quality. *A book is fiction by value if it deserves to be deeply ad-*

mired. Critics now believe—rightly or wrongly—that the books in the first list meet that description but that the books in the second do not. Any book in the first list may be termed fiction even if it is not fiction by intention, but no book in the second list will ever be called fiction unless it happens also to be fiction by intention.

If I am given a book I have never seen before I can tell pretty quickly whether critics will accept it as fiction by intention. I notice whether it (or at least its frame) is factually untrue and whether it has attached to it some signal of this from the author. But I am far from certain on the matter of its being accepted as fiction by value. Books I do not admire myself (e.g., Bronte's *Jane Eyre*) are generally accepted as fiction by value, and books I do admire (e.g., B. Traven's *Bridge in the Jungle*) are generally ignored. I am not even sure that when I do admire a book all other critics admire I am admiring it for the same reasons they are: certainly F. R. Leavis and Cleanth Brooks—the one a moral critic and the other a formalist—admired many of the same books but had wholly different standards for greatness, and I seem to read and judge somewhat differently from either of them.

Fiction by intention can be defined with moderately satisfactory precision, then: if we are still not sure precisely where the line between facts and generalizations exists in the critic's perceptions, we can at least make do with a broad smudge and call that a line. But the definition of fiction by value offers a wholly different problem: we still do not know *which* lines—however smudgy—ought to be drawn.

A book is a great book and therefore fiction by value if it "deserves to be deeply admired." But what will earn it that admiration? Critics and aestheticians have disagreed violently. Monroe C. Beardsley's list of seven theories found among aestheticians is instructive. 1] A great book "relieves tensions and quiets destructive impulses." 2] It "resolves lesser conflicts within the self, and helps to create an integration, or harmony." 3] It "refines perception and discrimination." 4] It "develops the imagination, and along with it the ability to put oneself in the place of others." 5] It is "an aid to mental health, but perhaps more as a preventive measure than as a cure." 6] It "fosters mutual sympathy and understanding." 7] It "offers an ideal for human life." [2] This is a list of explanations of what aestheticians call *the aesthetic experience*, but critics offer those explanations for greatness in literature too. (We ought, however, to add at least an eighth theory: 8] It gives us uniquely valuable insights into reality.) There are other theories being offered by critics, but the point is clear already. Even if we ignore those other theories — some of them as interesting as any of these — we still have to choose among eight different lines.

And it seems very unlikely anyway that there is only one distinction involved in the division between great and other books. We do know that books are deemed admirable and not-admirable by critics, and we know that critics have explained why they think them admirable. But, as I suggested earlier, when we compare those explanations we find that even two critics who agree as to the precise pitch of a book's value more often than not disagree as to *why* it should be praised that highly. There is good reason to suspect that a text may be valuable in any of a number of different ways and yet be accepted as fiction by value by critics. "It is important to remember the irrational diversity of our tastes," says N. W. Pirie, in quite another connection. "Even in Europe and the U. S. a flavor and appearance unacceptable in an egg is acceptable in cheese, a smell unacceptable in chicken is acceptable in pheasant or partridge, and a flavor unacceptable in wine is acceptable in grapefruit juice." [3]

To say that it is irrational to accept a certain taste in cheese and to reject it in eggs is to end all rational enquiry into the matter. It seems better to say that the standards of acceptability in foods are very complex and not easily reducible to verbal formulation. I think most scholars and many critics would feel that critics are no simpler in their literary tastes—no more predictable and describable—than they are when it comes to foods. But there is a further complication.

Every critic can name books he thinks admirable which he has not read. He is persuaded they are admirable because he knows they induced a state of admiration in other readers he respects. Critical appraisal takes place in a social context. The whole matter is far too complicated to be taken up here,[4] but this single matter of a critic's thinking admirable books he has not read can be taken as indicative of the kinds of problems a student of critical behavior faces. If each critic is too complex to be reduced to a simple formula that will allow us to predict precisely what he will feel about any new book, and if critics differ a good deal from one another, and if—in spite of this—critics also rely upon one another, then the class of the admirable for any single critic is very likely to contain books that *lack* features he privately requires of the admirable or even to manifest features he privately would take to eliminate a book from consideration as admirable. That should be plain enough: these books have induced a state of admiration in other critics that he can usually rely upon but—in these cases—at just the moments when he cannot rely upon them; he has not yet discovered this because he has not yet read the books. Until he has read them they will remain in the class of the admirable for him—misleading any student who would discover from study of the books he declares admirable what that critic's standards are.

It might be especially remarked that those books he

thinks admirable which are in languages he does not read or in disciplines unfamiliar to him may come recommended most persuasively by readers who are really quite different from him. Those who tell the critic that several Swahili epics meet the highest standards of literature are unlike that critic if only because they know Swahili and have almost certainly learned it in the process of acquiring quite a different education from his—in preparation for a career in anthropological or sociological or economic research, perhaps. Those who tell the critic that Newton's *Optics* is a book that deserves every human being's admiration are unlike the critic in that they have studied enough physics and mathematics so that they can read the *Optics*. What induces a state of wonder and approval in a Swahili-reader and a physicist who are offering advice to critics may be quite unlike anything that induces a state of admiration in the critic. It may be that the differences are not great enough to be important, but we do not yet know that. What we do know about this whole matter suggests that explanations of the admirable ought to be offered only with the most fearful tentativeness.

There is a question of intensity involved too. A book is fiction by value if it deserves to be *deeply* admired. How deeply? I can only suggest that it seems to vary a good deal from one critic to another. But one can feel a book is valuable without feeling it is greatly admirable and thus a part of fiction by value.

Our definition of fiction by value must be much shorter than our definition of fiction by intention—not because it is a simpler class but because it is less intelligible. We signal our ignorance by the simplicity of the definition: *a book is fiction by value if it deserves to be deeply admired*. How deeply? We do not know. In what ways? We are not sure. But we are sure of this: that the distinction between the admirable and the not-admirable is of immense importance to critics, and we can do some useful things even if we are certain only of that.

Most of the titles I have listed for fiction by value happen also to be recognized by critics as literature: Tolstoy's *Anna Karenina* and Boswell's *Life of Johnson* and Lucretius's *De rerum natura,* for instance. What relationship is there between literature and fiction by value? Is fiction by value just another name for literature, for instance? Or does all of literature fit under fiction by value? Or does all of fiction by value fit under literature?

The term literature is even more difficult to chart than is fiction, but it is quite plain that the two terms are not perfectly synonymous yet even though the one may be substituted for the other frequently. A glance at the list of books I gave as examples of works which are not a part of fiction by value will show immediately that some books recognized as literature appear there: Alfred Noyes's poem, "The Highwayman," for instance, may not be admired by critics but they would feel obscurely and reluctantly that it is a part of literature even if it is not fiction by value. And it would be a simple chore to add other titles of this kind: Longfellow's "The Village Blacksmith," for instance, and the play *Abie's Irish Rose* and William Hervey Allen's novel *Anthony Adverse.* The point to remark is that critics do not feel these works deserve to be deeply admired but do feel they are a part of literature in some way.

Nor is fiction by value merely a subdivision of literature for most critics, though the word literature is occasionally given the very broadest significance: a typical dictionary definition of the term declares it is "writings having excellence of form or expression and expressing ideas of permanent or universal interest" (*Webster's Third New International Dictionary*). But the critic almost always feels that the class of all literature merely intersects with the class of all books deserving to be deeply admired. He probably feels that those papers in which Einstein first presented his relativity theory deserve to be deeply admired, but he almost certainly feels they are not literature. It is better to think of fiction by value as having a literary part but also a nonliterary part too. I shall be returning to this question in the next chapter.

The outer boundaries of fiction by value are identical with the outer boundaries of a class we can call *great books*. If a book "deserves to be deeply admired" it is a great book. The first list of titles suggested that, but not very clearly; let us stop now to consider briefly the kinds of books critics are willing to admit are great. We think, of course, of books like Shakespeare's *Hamlet* and Dickens's *Hard Times* and Sterne's *Tristram Shandy* and Wordsworth's "Ode on Intimations of Immortality" and Meredith's *Modern Love* and Lawrence's *Lady Chatterley's Lover* and other instances of great literature. But we ought to remember, too, a great diversity of works that are thought of first in connection with the sciences and with history and with philosophy and with theology and with a hodgepodge of other activities pretty much outside the traditions of literature: the diary of Samuel Pepys, the sermons of John Donne, the histories of Prescott and Froude, and, of course, such other books as Charles Darwin's *Origin of Species* (biology), Jonathan Edwards's *Freedom of the Will* (theology), Locke's *An Essay Concerning Human Understanding* (philosophy), Joshua Reynolds's *Discourses* (art theory), Kingslake's *Eothen* (travel), Adam Smith's *Wealth of Nations* (economic theory) — the major bibliographies of English and American literature alone include hundreds of titles of works which seem admirable to the critic but outside the traditions usually thought central to literature. Critics themselves now tend to feel a bit awkward about slipping such titles into their reading lists for the courses in literature they teach, but they *do* get them into those reading lists—if necessary, under such headings as "Background" or "Other." In the essays critics write one finds oblique reference to them in terms that make it quite plain that the writer feels such books are admirable—whether he has read them or not.[5]

And so the class fiction by value is coterminous with the class great books. Why, then, am I not content to call it *great books*? Because fiction by value has a unique internal structure. It is convenient to have the word fiction in the name of the class when we are talking about the various uses of that word, of course, but that is not my principal reason for proposing this new label of mine. Fiction by value is coterminous with great books but so are other classes, and each of these classes has its own internal structure, its own characteristic division into subclasses.

One example: I shall be talking a little later about the parallels to be drawn between the critic's use of the word fiction and his use of the word poetry. As it happens, he uses the word poetry in two different but related ways also. Sometimes he has it refer to a class we might call *poetry by intention*, which is merely the class *verse*. And sometimes he has it refer to all or parts of the class great books: if he is willing to call Gibbon's *Decline and Fall of the Roman Empire* a great fiction he is also sometimes willing to call it a great poem. But his use of the word poetry in connection with great books does not precisely match his use of the word fiction there. For instance, while the critic using the word fiction identifies great novels as central to all great books in that connection, he identifies great lyrics as central when he is deploying the word poetry. Great books have one articulation for the critic when he is using the word fiction, they have another articulation when he is using the word poetry. The same class subdivided variously needs different labels. Hence the terms fiction by value and (potentially) such other terms as poetry by value and drama by value and literature by value and so forth. Fiction by value is the class great books conceived of as having a unique hierarchy of subclasses.

These, then, are the difficulties anyone faces who tries to determine precisely where the boundaries between the great and the nongreat lie. But one difficulty remains to be considered, and it is by no means the least. A simple noncritical view of the matter would have it that the books critics think great are merely those that happen to affect them deeply. If this were the case it would follow that I, for instance, might discover what greatness in books is for critics by taking a critic, determining which books do have a profound emotional impact on him, and then through analysis and corroboratory experiment discover what it is in those books that is triggering that emotional experience in him. The result: a permanent definition of literature as critics see it.

But that is not the problem at all. We have said that fiction by value (and great books and poetry by value and so on) includes all books that deserve to be deeply admired. The word *deserve*, in this definition, is of great qualifying importance, for the distinction between the book that *is* admired, the book that *might* be admired, and the book that *deserves* to be admired is everything in criticism. The procedure just outlined—where we would select a critic and determine what is triggering that special kind of excitement in him—would tell us only what in a book elicits his admiration, but our problem is to determine what it is that makes him feel a book *deserves* an admiration he may or may not actually feel for it.

Admiration is "a sentiment of wonder, approval,

pleasure, excited by contemplation of beauty, skill, merit, or excellence of any kind." If I *do* admire a book —Traven's *Bridge in the Jungle*, let us say—then a reading of that book creates in me that sentiment of wonder, approval, etc. It may be that I do not admire a book and yet recognize that others do. I do not admire Grace Metalious's novel *Peyton Place* though I do recognize that many did admire it in its day; I do not admire Charles Dickens's *David Copperfield* but of course I know that most critics who have read it do admire it.

I think it must be obvious enough that the class of all great books does not for the critic include all the books that *could* be admired: that would have it include all the books that ever have been or ever could be written. Nor does it include all the books that *have* been admired: the critic does not include *Peyton Place* among the great books of Western civilization; he does not feel that those who admired *Peyton Place* were competent to make sound literary judgments. No one has missed this aspect of literary criticism.

What is apparently less evident—though critics themselves are never in doubt on the matter—is that a book's failure to put even a critic himself into a state of admiration does not by itself convince him the book is not a great book. And if a book should happen to put him into a state of admiration, he does not automatically assume it must be great. People who imagine that critics suppose that all books that awe them are great books and that no books that do not awe them are great seriously misunderstand the complexities of literary criticism. The individual critic is much humbler about his own competence as a reader than is usually credited. He has a keen sense of his own limitations as a reader. I can illustrate this aspect of criticism, at least, by reference to some of my own attitudes. I first read P. C. Wren's novels about the French Foreign Legion when I was a child and took a huge delight in them. Even today I find that I can recapture some of that admiration I felt then. So I cannot deny that I do admire them, and yet I do not press them on my friends in the way I do Euclides da Cunha's *Os Sertoes*, a book I also admire. As it happens, I have never studied the poetry of William Blake deeply enough to feel fully at ease with his later work, and I can read through *The Book of Urizen* and *Milton* without feeling more than a shadow of the awed fascination the student of Blake feels when he reads them. But I identify myself as incompetent in this case: I am persuaded that they deserve more admiration than I can honestly claim to feel for them. And in these two cases I am merely typical of literary critics generally.

Fiction by value, then, includes for any critic only those books he thinks deserve to be deeply admired. True, it does include most of the books he does actually admire, but it also includes many he does not actually admire: many books he has never even read and many others he feels he does not read properly. And some of the books he does actually admire do not seem to him to belong to that group. It includes only those he thinks he *should* admire. How is he persuaded that he should admire a certain book but not admire some other? We do not know that either. We do not yet understand how critics become convinced they should admire certain books. We do not yet know which kinds of admiration they do actually associate with greatness in books. And we do not know how intensely they must admire something before they will identify it as great. If we knew these things we might hope to write a more precise definition—as precise, at least, as the one we can write for fiction by intention.

But we can make do with less. We do know that critics use such phrases as *masterpieces* and *great* and *supreme achievement* and *eternal* when talking about books: we know that they do distinguish between a class of books they think are great and other books of less or no merit. And we do know that they deploy the term fiction in reference to various parts of this class.

A more careful explanation of fiction by value would tell us that *critics identify a text as fiction by value when they are persuaded it deserves to be deeply admired.* But the simpler definition will serve just about as well:

A book is fiction by value when it deserves to be deeply admired.

4

The Structure of Fifv

Fifv is the superclass whose major divisions are fiction by value and fiction by intention. Anything which is either fiction by value or fiction by intention or both is a part of fifv. If a book deserves to be deeply admired or if its writer knowingly made it factually untrue but also warned his reader he had done this or if—like Fielding's *Tom Jones* and Joyce's *Ulysses* and Dostoevsky's *The Brothers Karamazov* and Austen's *Emma*—it meets both sets of criteria it is in fifv. If it is within the boundaries of fifv it may be named fiction at one time or another; if it is not, it will never be named fiction by critics.

It is also the case that the word fiction is never given all of the meaning I am giving the word fifv. Nor, for that matter, is any other word ever given all of the meaning I am giving fifv; if there were such a word, I would be using it instead of fifv. We are interested in fifv only because its outer boundaries represent the outer limits of the many different uses of the word fiction.

The word fiction is sometimes used to refer to all of fiction by intention and it is sometimes (but rarely) used to refer to all of fiction by value. If these two were the only uses given the word, the mapping of its use would be much simpler than it is. Actually, the word is at one moment used to refer to only part of fiction by intention and at another to refer to only part of fiction by value, and this forces us to consider the divisions indigenous to each of those two classes and also the divisions created by their intersection. This will involve me in several elaborately nice distinctions, but I think it is worth the effort to understand them. We end with a useful insight into the concept-structures most basic to literary criticism, and we understand better than we did why so much literary theory is so bafflingly difficult to understand.

The word fiction has nine different though related meanings. Each is a part of fifv. Here are the nine meanings I shall be identifying. Three are parts of fiction by intention, three others are parts of fiction by value, and three others (the ones italicized below and listed twice) are members of both classes.

Fiction by Intention

1. Fiction by intention. (*Great fiction by intention.*)
2. Prose fiction by intention. (*Great prose fiction by intention.*)
3. Novels. (*Great novels.*)

Fiction by Value

4. Great books.
5. Great literature.
6. Great imaginative literature.
7. *Great fiction by intention.*
8. *Great prose fiction by intention.*
9. *Great novels.*

As far as the word fiction is concerned, fiction by intention is divided into six classes, and fiction by value is divided into six classes, and—as I have already observed —three classes are held in common by the two major classes.

Fiction by Intention. If the writer of a book knowingly made it factually untrue but also warned his reader he had done this, that book is fiction by intention. Any book we find that fits that description will seem to critics to be fiction in at least some extended use of the term, whether the book is good or bad, whether it is in prose or verse, whether it has a plot or is simply a sketch. The largest meaning fiction is given when it is used with a fiction-by-intention orientation, then, is just the meaning 'fiction by intention.'

But the word is not always used in that largest fiction-by-intention sense. Sometimes it is used in narrower senses, and to understand those narrower senses we must recognize two distinctions critics make among the various instances of fiction by intention. The first is the distinction between prose and verse, and the second is the distinction between books having a narrative element and those which lack it.

Verse is metrical composition as distinct from non-metrical composition, which is prose. I am not introducing a poetry/prose distinction: perhaps "Thirty Days Hath September" is not a poem, but it is verse; perhaps Jonathan Edwards's sermon, "Sinners in the Hands of an Angry God" *is* a poem, but it is not verse. The distinctions between verse and prose are not nearly so clear as we usually take them to be—the prose of Lyly's *Euphues* is more metrical than is vers libre, and yet we continue to call it prose and the latter verse—but the line between the two is still much firmer than is, say, the line between great and lesser books. Obviously, critics do distinguish between prose and verse and rarely find themselves in disagreement on the matter. It will also be obvious that a work of fiction by intention may be in either prose or verse: Noyes's poem, "The Highwayman," for instance, is in verse and yet fiction by intention, Poe's story, "The Masque of the Red Death," is fiction by intention and prose.

The addition of the prose/verse distinction to our distinction between fiction by intention and everything else offers no special difficulty, but we will be adding distinctions to this one later and small difficulties compound one another, and I want to obviate as much of the later difficulties as I can. Imagine, then, that we have drawn a largish rectangle on a sheet of paper and that we are taking it to represent the class fiction by intention: all books inside that rectangle are fiction by intention, all outside it are not. We can draw another rectangle of about the same size and have it overlap that first rectangle and label the second rectangle *prose*. Now we have two kinds of fiction by intention—prose and verse —and two parallel kinds of not–fiction by intention. But we are going to ignore, at least for a while, everything which is not fiction-by-intention, so let us make that second rectangle smaller than the first and put it inside the first. The second rectangle is—again—prose, and we have now created three classes: the class of all fiction by intention, to which we have already devoted ample time, and the class of prose fiction by intention, and the class of verse fiction by intention.

The prose portion of fiction by intention is more central now to the concepts critics have of fiction than the verse portion. If a critic were asked to list some examples of books he would name fiction, for instance, he would probably begin by listing novels and short stories written during the past two centuries: Tolstoy's *Anna Karenina*, Mark Twain's *Huckleberry Finn*, Fielding's *Tom Jones*, Susann's *The Love Machine*, Metalious's *Peyton Place*, and Mitchell's *Gone With the Wind* are novels he might very well list, some thought admirable and others not. Eudora Welty's "Petrified Man," Poe's "Murders in the Rue Morgue," O. Henry's "The Gift of the Magi," Faulkner's "Spotted Horses," the stories in Joyce's *Dubliners* and in Anderson's *Winesburg, Ohio* are familiar enough representatives of the short story.

Since the critic has shown increasing interest in novellas, these are very likely to appear high on his list: Melville's *Benito Cereno*, James's *The Turn of the Screw*, Conrad's *The Secret Sharer*, Kafka's *Metamorphosis*, and so forth. But the class also includes, for him, the many prose forerunners of the novel—the Greek romances, most of the tales in *The Thousand and One Nights* and in Boccaccio's *Decameron*, Malory's *Mort d'Arthur*, and countless thousands of other prose stories. We think of all these prose texts as telling stories, but there are other members of the class that do not seem to the critic to be narrative. These present us with fictional personas; Charles Lamb's *Essays of Elia* will serve as an example, and Peter Finley Dunne's *Mr. Dooley's Philosophy* and Oliver Wendell Holmes's "The Autocrat of the Breakfast Table." In the strictest interpretation of the class, prose fiction by intention also includes what is perhaps (in the United States, at least) the most common, the most complex, and yet the least studied of all the forms fiction by intention takes—the popular jokes that pass by word of mouth from one person to another. I suspect literary critics never do have these stories about traveling salesmen, about presidential candidates and their wives, about Jewish logicians, etc., in mind when they use the word fiction, but these jokes clearly do meet the criteria for fiction by intention listed and I shall leave the question of the critics' unconscious awareness of them to someone else.

No one will need to be reminded of such works as Robert Service's "The Shooting of Dan McGrew," Alfred Noyes's "The Highwayman," Coleridge's "The Ancient Mariner," and Robert Frost's "The Witch of Coös." These works and many thousands like them are instances of fiction by intention in verse, as are such nonnarrative works as Christopher Marlowe's "The Passionate Shepherd to His Love," T. S. Eliot's "The Love

Song of J. Alfred Prufrock," and Robert Browning's "My Last Duchess," all of which present fictional personas. Today it is felt that the prose portion is somehow or other more central to fiction by intention and that the verse portion is more central to poetry, but it seems probable that this is one of the many side effects of the rise of the novel in the nineteenth century. In the Renaissance, when the term poetry was explained in pretty much the way fiction is explained today, the verse instances of fiction by intention were felt to be central.

Are plays fiction by intention? Clearly, plays like George Bernard Shaw's *Man and Superman* and Oscar Wilde's *The Importance of Being Earnest* are prose and also fiction by intention and thus presumably already covered, and plays like Shakespeare's *King Lear* and Dryden's *All for Love* are verse and fiction by intention and might have been listed with the verse "The Shooting of Dan McGrew" and "The Ancient Mariner." Now, whether we think of these plays as *scripts* or as *performances*, it seems likely that we would identify them as fiction by intention, but the distinction between the script and the performance may in other cases be important. While it does seem that a script may or may not be fiction by intention (in prose or in verse), yet it does seem to me that a performance could not be anything except fiction by intention. For even if I were to make a script by copying an exact transcript of what some people had said on some historic occasion, when actors spoke those lines they would give them their own inflections and pace and they would accompany them with gestures and movements that they had invented themselves, and it seems to me that these inflections and gestures, etc., would meet the criteria I found characteristic of fiction by intention (the actors would feel they were literally untrue and would expect their audiences to know this). Thus I would argue that while the

script may or may not be fiction by intention, the performance is always fiction by intention. This is not a
question that concerns literary criticism, however, and
I pass it by, noting that the newer forms of the theater
(e.g., the "happenings") do make the question rather
more difficult to settle than it was only a few years ago.

We are much less sure of ourselves on the distinctions
between narratives and nonnarratives than we are on
the distinctions between prose and verse. And yet it is
important that we introduce this distinction. Let us set
aside the problem of distinguishing between *story* and
plot and say, somewhat evasively, that a narrative is a
work which gives an account of a sequence of events:
Faulkner's "A Rose for Emily" is a narrative but
Holmes's "The Autocrat of the Breakfast Table" is not;
"The Rime of the Ancient Mariner" is a narrative, but
"The Love Song of J. Alfred Prufrock" is somehow or
other not a narrative.

Back to that diagram we had begun to construct. We
already have one large rectangle (fiction by intention)
and inside it a smaller rectangle (prose fiction by intention). Let us introduce a yet smaller rectangle (narratives) inside the second. We might call this last *prose
narrative fiction by intention,* but that is a difficult label
to juggle and I will call it, less clearly but more conveniently, *novels.* When something is fiction by intention and is also in prose and is also a narrative, it must
be a play in prose or a short story or a short novel or a
romance or a novel. If we take the label *novels* to include
all of those different kinds, we will avoid some very
clumsy terminology.[1]

The three rectangles we have drawn represent three of
the nine meanings of the word fiction. This should not
require elaborate proof. 1) Critics often use the word
fiction to refer to all those things we find in our class
novels, but only to those things. 2) Sometimes the

word has a larger meaning: it refers to everything we call novels but also to any other prose fiction by intention, whether it is a narrative or not. In this extended sense, Dunne's *Mr. Dooley's Philosophy* is fiction, though in the previous sense of the term it is not: it is then referred to rather awkwardly as a collection of sketches or as comic philosophy or with some other term that does not highlight those features we have been considering. 3) Sometimes, again, the word has the largest of these three meanings. It refers then to novels and to non-narrative prose fiction by intention as well but also to any verse fiction by intention (whether it is a narrative or not).

These are the only three of the nine meanings of fiction which are wholly nonevaluative. Agatha Christie's *Murder in the Calais Coach* is not thought of as a great book but it is a part of fiction in any of the three senses identified so far. When discussing the various classes found in fiction by value we shall begin by cutting each of these three meanings into two parts and will then have three new meanings of the nine we shall eventually consider.

Before turning to fiction by value, however, consider the great variety of classes we have *not* examined. If we drew a diagram which had three large rectangles overlapping one another we would see better the larger relationships obtaining among the classes prose and narrative and fiction by intention. One of the eight classes identified for us would be verse narrative fiction by intention, a counterclass, if you will, to the class novels. It seems likely that it is just this class Sir Philip Sidney had in mind when he used the word poetry as an approximate synonym for our word fiction. He does not always reduce the word's meaning to this narrowest sense (for he does accept Plato's *Dialogues* as belonging to the class at one point), but he and his contemporaries were more intrigued by the verse than they were by the prose they knew. It is probably not until late in the nineteenth century, in England and the United States at any rate, that the novel achieved the kind of centrality it currently has. This probably goes a long way to explain why it is that when we want a synonym for the word literature we increasingly turn to the word fiction rather than to the word poetry with its connotation of verse.

Fiction by Value. We now have a nest of three meanings and will examine another nest with which it intersects. Fiction by value, it may be remembered, is the class great books perceived as having a certain internal structure: it is one of several classes coterminous (in the mind of the critic) with the class great books. The differences in structure among these several classes arise because of the different classes with which great books intersects. When great books intersects with the class fiction by intention, it inevitably has a different structure —that is, *is* a different nest of meanings—than it is when it intersects with the class verse or the class plays.

It is convenient to think of fiction by value as having two major divisions. I shall speak of an outer structure and of an inner structure. Each is a nest of three meanings. The inner structure of fiction by value is unique; but it shares its outer structure with other classes coterminous with great books. We will study the inner structure first.

The inner structure of fiction by value is intricate but it can be grasped immediately by means of that diagram we have been preparing. In that diagram, we now have the class novels inside the class prose fiction by intention inside the class fiction by intention as a whole: our diagram represents them as a nest of three rectangles. Think of that nest of rectangles as drawn vertically on the page: lying across it horizontally and overlapping its upper part is the other rectangle with which it forms that capital *T* which is the class fifv. Let us suppose that the lower line of the horizontal rectangle marks the distinction between great and lesser books within fiction by intention. Anything above that line (and inside that horizontal rectangle, fiction by value) is a great book, anything below that line is not.

The horizontal line has divided the three classes we started with into six classes: there is, for instance, great fiction by intention and less-than-great fiction by intention and so forth. The only classes that interest us, however, are those above the line. There are three of them, and they too are nested. They make up the inner structure of fiction by value, and they are meanings four, five, and six of the word fiction. Indeed, they are the most important meanings of all.

By dividing the earlier class novels into the great and the less-than-great, we have isolated the class *great novels.* Our label novels included *Moby-Dick*, a great book, but it also included books like Agatha Christie's *Murder in the Calais Coach*, it will be recalled, and all the other novels, short stories, short novels, and prose plays that are in prose and are narratives and are fiction by intention but which do not seem to the critic to deserve to be deeply admired. The critic always feels a kind of reluctant loyalty to books of this latter type (who will cherish them if he will not?), but his most central commitment has been, in the recent past at least, to that relatively small number among them which he feels are truly great: precisely to Melville's *Moby-Dick* and Hawthorne's *The Scarlet Letter* and Joyce's *Ulysses* and Eliot's *Middlemarch* and Austen's *Emma* and Richardson's *Clarissa* and Joyce's "The Dead" and Welty's "Why I Live at the P.O." and Faulkner's "That Evening Sun" and Kafka's *The Great Wall of China* and Dostoevsky's *Notes from Underground* and Chekhov's *The Cherry*

Orchard and Ibsen's *Hedda Gabler* and O'Neill's *Long Day's Journey into Night* and the others to which he gives his time and faith and energy. This is the class great novels, and it is the core meaning of the word fiction; I shall have much to say about it in a moment.

Our earlier class, prose fiction by intention, has now had identified within it a subclass, *great prose fiction by intention*, which happens to include great novels as well as, for instance, the comic essays of Josh Billings and Artemus Ward, which have little that is narrative within them but most typically intrigue us through the revelations of a personality of quite incredible ignorance and yet no small intelligence. The smaller class is unlike the larger class in which we find it in that it does not include any narrative or nonnarrative fiction by intention in prose which is not of the highest quality: it does not include the westerns of Clarence Mulford, say, and the comic essays of Irvin S. Cobb.

And fiction by intention itself has now been reduced to *great fiction by intention*, which includes both the earlier classes but also all great verse which is fiction by intention whether it be narrative or not: it includes, then, Coleridge's "The Rime of the Ancient Mariner," but not such works as Noyes's "The Highwayman."

Fiction is a word which means 'great novels' and also means 'great novels and other books significantly like them.' We have now identified five of the ways in which that word fiction may be extended out to "other books significantly like" great novels. We shall very shortly be adding three additional extensions of the word, but we have enough now so that we can begin to see how one key term in literary criticism maintains its identity and yet expands and contracts as the critic finds that convenient. The narrowest meaning the word fiction can have is that core meaning, 'great novels.' Whatever else the word may mean on any occasion, it always means at least that. This is of essential importance.

Words like literature and fiction and poetry and drama (and also words like art and science and religion in nonliterary groups) are so slippery that it is only after we have encountered each one some hundreds of times that we begin to sense that we are no longer encountering new extensions of their meanings. But when we choose to concentrate on one of those terms and do begin to isolate the meanings, we find that they overlap and incorporate and exclude and confirm and contradict one another in so confused a tangle that we feel we are not much better off than we were before. We feel there must be pattern or that critics would not understand one another, but we begin to despair of ever finding a single pattern, however complex, and we begin to wonder whether critics actually do understand—or even listen to—one another.

Eventually I discovered what I suppose many another has discovered for himself before me: that if I ask myself whether there is anything at all that the term always refers to, anything everyone feels it *ought* always refer to, I can usually find some class of texts or genres that fits that description. Literary critics are very tolerant about the uses of the word fiction, and none of them would object if he heard me use the word to refer to great prose fiction by intention and rather obviously deny that any verse is fiction—even Keats's "La Belle Dame Sans Merci" or Spenser's *The Faerie Queene*. He might very well not choose himself ever to use the word in just that way, but he is prepared to hear others use it that way without protest. And he will not blink if on another occasion he hears me use the word to refer to all novels —great and less than great—but not, for some reason, to any verse or any prose nonnarratives. It is as though I had used a hammer one day to pound a nail and the next to crack open a walnut: for him, the word fiction is a tool that can be used in various ways. But if I were to use the word fiction and made it quite clear that I did not intend to refer to such books as George Eliot's *Silas Marner* and Thackeray's *Vanity Fair* and Chekhov's "The Kiss" and Tolstoy's *The Death of Ivan Ilyich,* then he and all other critics who heard me would think it very odd indeed. Whatever else fiction is, critics feel, it has something to do with those books, and anyone who does not feel it involves those books very sadly misunderstands it. Which is to say that for critics the word fiction does "really" mean 'great novels' always even if it means more than that too.

But often it means 'great novels and other books significantly like them'; and which other books *do* seem significantly like great novels to the critic? We have already identified part of the answer to that question, of course. Sometimes the other books significantly like great novels are all other novels, even those that are not great. Sometimes they are all other instances of fiction by intention. Sometimes they are only all other instances of great fiction by intention. And so forth.

It is possible that at the heart of the critic's notion of literature—whatever he might name that field of books and writing traditions which draws his loyalty—is a small system of core meanings like the one we have found for the word fiction. These are the meanings on which such words as poetry and drama depend most heavily. It would be very difficult to prove that it has happened, but I suspect that essential changes in the notions of literature occur precisely there—among these core meanings. Take what seems to be the case of the word poetry. To Sir Philip Sidney the word poetry had a core meaning which we can identify in our terminology as 'great verse narrative fiction by intention.' (We would probably be calling that earlier core meaning *great epics*—with as many embarrassed reservations as we have for the term great novels.) As we have already seen, he did think of the Platonic dialogues as poetry and so we know he did

not confine the term only to verse, and yet everything
we know about that period suggests that he would have
thought of poetry as most centrally connected with objects which are fiction by intention and are narratives
and are verse rather than prose. The core meaning of the
word poetry is different today. As I shall explain later,
that core meaning seems to be 'great lyrics,' and the word
now has only loose connections with the concept of fiction by intention. And so there is evident a shift in core
meaning for a single word. But there is more of interest
in this phenomenon than just that. For the term fiction
has emerged with its own core meaning, which is not
the one the term poetry used to have. It is true that in
our use of the word fiction there is an emphasis on that
curious admitted lying which is characteristic of fiction
by intention and that in Sidney's use of the word poetry
there is that same emphasis, and it is true that he would
sometimes have used the word poetry to indicate things
we label fiction, but a man who bases his thinking on
verse narrative fiction by intention has a subtly different
mind than one who bases it on prose narrative fiction by
intention.

Our core meaning, 'great novels,' plays a significant
role in the deployment of the word fiction, first, because
it is in all the various meanings the word ever has and,
second, because it is a part of fiction by intention and is
also a part of fiction by value. Fiction by intention is a
class defined wholly by formal criteria: anything, good
or bad, is fiction by intention if its writer thought it factually untrue and warned his reader of that. Fiction by
value is a class defined in value terms: a book is fiction
by value if it deserves to be deeply admired. George
Eliot's *Middlemarch* is a great novel and is therefore
characterized by both wholly formal and wholly evaluative criteria. When we use the word fiction with emphasis on this smallest class, we can have in mind as

most significant about it either its evaluative characteristics or any of its formal characteristics. And that is where the difficulty or, if you like, the special advantage of this type of concept-structure lies.

That very simple diagram we began with many pages ago had two large rectangles crossing one another to form a plain capital *T*, and it had the class great novels as a very small rectangle inside the area of overlap. (The two other parts of the inner structure of fiction by value we have just located are also in this area, but the class great novels appears at their center.) When it is not regarded as improper that the word fiction be allowed to pivot on this one class, the critic can do wonders in the defense of fiction—and bewilder us and himself hopelessly at the same time. Consider the possibilities.

I am a critic, let us say, whose chief interest in literature happens to be in that group of works we are calling great novels; I am fascinated and awed by the novels of Melville and Austen and Thackeray and Richardson and by the short stories of D. H. Lawrence and Ernest Hemingway and Anton Chekhov and Nathaniel Hawthorne and by the plays of August Strindberg and Henrik Ibsen and Jean Genêt, and so on. When I think of fiction, I think of these works. But I also feel an obscure and half-unwilling loyalty to all novels and short stories and plays even if they are so bad I despise them. I attack those bad novels and short stories and plays when I am with other critics, but I feel called upon to defend them when people who are not critics attack them. And I do defend them, for I feel that fiction is very important. For, I remind myself, fiction includes such works as Melville's "Bartleby the Scrivener" and Fielding's *Tom Jones* and Chekhov's *The Three Sisters* and those are immensely important. And it includes, I continue, Milton's *Paradise Lost* and Wordsworth's Lucy poems and Burton's *Anatomy of Melancholy* and Gibbon's *Decline and*

Fall of the Roman Empire and even Darwin's *Origin of Species* and the works of Aquinas and Aristotle. And if it includes the eminently forgettable novels of Mary Roberts Rinehart, those who would attack these last novels might forget that much of tremendous importance still remains in the class.

Since the word fiction is linked to the concept-structure we have identified, this kind of reasoning seems curiously plausible—at least, to the person who is doing that reasoning. And there are two features to be remarked. The first is that half-unwilling loyalty of which he cannot rid himself even though he despises bad novels much more than anyone who is not a critic can know, much more than they can despise them because they do not take the novel as seriously as he does. Why does he feel that dim loyalty? It is a function of his acceptance of the critics' concept-structure. He is deeply committed to the great novels, but he names them fiction and that label implicates him in weaker spheres of commitment to everything else called fiction—for instance, to the whole of fiction by intention.

The second is the reasoning which assures him that fiction should not be denigrated ever. Let us suppose it is Jaqueline Susann's *Valley of the Dolls* which the noncritic is using as an excuse to challenge the whole enterprise of novel-writing. The critic who despises that novel identifies it as fiction because it is prose narrative fiction by intention. But he is confident that fiction is important. Hemingway's *The Sun Also Rises* is a prose narrative in fiction by intention, for instance, and it is important: so generalizations on fiction drawn from novels like Susann's *Valley of the Dolls* are mistaken. And at this point, with his attention focused on those novels and short stories he deeply admires, it is possible that the word fiction will shrink in meaning in his own mind to merely 'great novels.' Once this has occurred, it

is possible for the meaning to expand in a new direction
—out into fiction by value. So the critic recognizes on
second thought that fiction includes not only that Hemingway novel but also works like Milton's *Paradise Lost*
—which is unlike *The Valley of the Dolls* in that it is neither prose nor fiction by intention but which is fiction in
the sense 'great fiction by intention.' And having made
the pivot from a fiction-by-intention orientation to a
fiction-by-value orientation, the critic may find himself
now giving the word fiction a further extension in meaning so as to include all great books—and then it refers as
well to the writings of Aquinas and of Darwin and many
other books not very much like *The Valley of the Dolls*
at all. This is a very common event in literary criticism,
and it is hardly surprising that we often baffle even ourselves with the chains of thought we invoke. The critic
need only be a little careless in his verbalizations and
thought, a little less than scrupulous at key moments,
and those small shifts and transformations have occurred. And as we have seen, it is not always to the
critic's advantage: the ambiguity in the meanings of
fiction do also burden the critic with loyalties he would
rather not feel.

I do not want to leave anyone with the impression
that I suppose this kind of reasoning is found only in
literary criticism. I can testify to having read some years
ago an essay in defense of that European music we
Americans call *classical*. The writer's essay was in two
parts; the first was a defense and the second a celebra-
tion of the works he most loved. He began his defense
by asserting that a complex work is superior to a simple
one. He then showed us that the sonata form of the
nineteenth-century symphony is more complex than the
march and ballad forms characteristic of earlier
twentieth-century jazz. With patient good humor and
quiet satisfaction, he then concluded, for us, that clas-

sical music is superior to jazz. In the second part of his essay he told—in a very human way—of the pleasures he took in the works he most admired, which proved to be not symphonies at all but operatic arias, art songs, and program music of the more obvious kind. For that writer (and he is certainly not unique), classical music means only the great symphonies and chamber music when anyone brings its value into question; but once it has been established that classical music is good, the meaning of the phrase expands to include even the simplest works composed within that tradition.

'Great novels' is the core meaning of the word fiction. It may also be termed a *pivot* meaning. We have seen how fiction can shift from an evaluative to a nonevaluative significance when we are thinking of fiction as being wholly a matter of texts. But the word may pivot from a texts-orientation to a genre-orientation, too; I shall go into that later.

The outer part of fiction by value is much less important in the use of the word fiction than is the inner part, but the word is sometimes used synonymously with the word literature and then the outer part has its role to play, too. Back to our diagram. The inner part of fiction by value is a nest of three rectangles also inside fiction by intention just where fiction by value and fiction by intention intersect. The outer part of fiction by value is a nest of three rectangles which has the inner part at its center. The largest rectangle is *great books*. (As I said earlier I am reserving the term fiction by value to suggest the class great books as subdivided in one unique way.) If the diagram is so constructed that this nest of three rectangles making up the outer part surrounds the upper portion of fiction by intention (that is, that nest of three rectangles which is the inner portion of fiction by value), the relations among the various meanings are immediately apparent. As we have already seen, the word fiction is extended out along either of two axes: a fiction-by-intention axis or a fiction-by-value axis. We are forced to examine this outer part of fiction by value because the word is sometimes extended beyond the limits of fiction by intention.

The diagram itself is simple enough, once it has been drawn correctly, but the relations among the various parts of fiction by value that we have to consider are rather intricate. The diagram is useful in telling us about the various extensions of the word fiction but it has been simplified radically to suggest little more than that. In order to understand what each of these three new rectangles represents we shall have to look at them very closely.

Let us begin with that largest rectangle. I am calling this great books. It has, for our purposes, two parts. The first of them includes all great books which critics do not think literature: I have been citing Charles Darwin's *Origin of Species* as an example of this group. The other part of great books includes all that are literature. I shall be referring to this with the familiar phrase, *great literature*. This happens to be the second of the three rectangles that make up the inner part of fiction by value.

The rectangle great literature is also divided into two parts. There is no word or phrase currently in use which unambiguously identifies either class, and so I shall offer two of my own. I shall call the first part of great literature *great nonimaginative literature* and the second part *great imaginative literature*. The smallest rectangle of the three in the nest is *great imaginative literature*; it contains great fiction by intention and also great plays and great verse.

Meanings seven, eight, and nine of the word fiction, then, are 'great imaginative literature,' 'great literature,' and 'great books.' The seventh meaning is a part of the eighth and both are a part of the ninth meaning.

Great imaginative literature. This is the smallest class in the outer part of fiction by value, but it does include within it all of the inner part—all of great fiction by intention. The name was suggested to me by some sentences C. S. Lewis wrote.

> I am theorizing not about art in general but about literature; and not even about all literature, but about imaginative literature—about poetry, drama, and the novel. I am prepared to grant that there are writings, and writings properly called literature, whose value consists in the impression they give us of the writer's personality. Private letters are obviously in this class; and many essays are also in it.[2]

It is characteristic of critics in general that they feel certain kinds of books are more central to literature than others. They have a much greater interest in those more central kinds and feel a somewhat fiercer loyalty to them. Further, the word *imaginative* is one that critics like to apply to literature, and there seems to be no particularly good reason why we should not follow Lewis's usage. And, finally, the genres that do most interest critics are the ones he refers to as "poetry, drama, and the novel." I shall follow C. S. Lewis's distinctions, then—not because he is authoritative but because he seems to be typical. I shall make some slight changes in terminology. Instead of speaking of poetry and drama and the novel —all of which are ambiguously purely formal or formal/ evaluative terms—I shall speak of verse and plays and fiction by intention.

If it is not wholly certain, it seems a reasonable inference that Lewis's imaginative literature includes even trivial verse and trivial plays and trivial fiction by intention. But I am interested in only that part of the class which is within fiction by value. I have therefore put the adjective *great* in front of Lewis's phrase to get the label *great imaginative literature.*

One of the three categories within great imaginative literature is great fiction by intention, then, and the others are great verse and great plays. (I myself feel that since plays are either in verse or in prose they are already accounted for when we have named those two forms, but it is a custom to name the three separately.) In the six meanings of fiction we have already examined, the books referred to are always fiction by intention. This seventh meaning of the word—'great imaginative literature'—is the first we have encountered in which the word refers to books which are outside the limits of fiction by intention. For Milton's *Paradise Lost* is great imaginative literature, but it is not fiction by intention. And Pope's *Essay on Man* is fiction in this sense, too, but it is not fiction by intention.

Great literature and *great books*. It is easy enough to distinguish between great imaginative literature, on the one hand, and great books, on the other: any book that deserves to be deeply admired is a great book but it is not part of that smaller class unless it is in verse or is a play or is in fiction by intention. Perhaps that is the only distinction needed? The word fiction is often used to refer to great imaginative literature, and it is sometimes used to refer to great books. But my sense of the uses of the word suggests that there is one further distinction made.

Eliminate from consideration all great books that are verse or plays or fiction by intention. This still leaves us with an immense number: we have Gibbon's *Decline and Fall of the Roman Empire* and Kingslake's *Eothen* and Edwards's *Freedom of the Will* and Locke's *An Essay Concerning Human Understanding* and the essays of Addison and Steele and the letters of Horace Walpole, and also the writings of Albert Einstein and Charles Darwin and C. S. Peirce and other scientists and philosophers. Critics are pretty generally agreed that all of these books deserve our deep admiration, though I think they would not agree that they should all be lumped together under such a phrase as Lewis's "literature of personality." But they also recognize some distinctions among them which are relevant to their uses of the word fiction.

I find three classes which I shall later reduce to two. The first class includes those books written in traditions which critics do recognize as essentially literary but which they feel are less central to literature than the traditions of verse and plays and fiction by intention. The second class includes books written in traditions which are *not* essentially literary. These books have been adopted into literature on the basis of merit. The third class includes all those books which deserve our deep admiration but which are not recognized as literature even by adoption. The first two classes with great imaginative literature make up great literature. The third class is outside great literature but combines with it to make up great books.

Critics do recognize certain traditions of writing in prose—the personal essay and the letter, most notably—which are somehow or other literary and yet also somehow or other less central to literature than verse and plays and fiction by intention. The essays of Charles Lamb, the autobiography in such a form as *The Education of Henry Adams*, travel narratives like Kingslake's *Eothen* and Doughty's *Travels in Arabia Deserta* and perhaps even such efforts in literary criticism as Coleridge's *Biographia Literaria* and Dryden's *Essay of Dramatic Poesy* are hailed as great and also—but less certainly—as literature. Call this *great marginal literature*, with the word *marginal* suggesting only that the traditions in which these books were written are felt not quite so surely literary as the three traditions in great imaginative literature. This is the part of literature which is most usefully characterized with C. S. Lewis's phrase, the literature of personality.[3]

All of the great books that remain to be considered are in nonliterary traditions. But some of them have come to be accepted by critics as literature by adoption. Many critics have remarked on this. Here is Graham Hough in his *Essay on Criticism*:

> It has also become apparent that in attempting to delimit literature we make use of two distinctions, one qualitative and the other evaluative. We distinguish literature as a special kind of discourse—fictional or imaginary discourse; and we also say that other kinds of discourse may become literature by special merit.[4]

There are those central literary kinds and then other, more peripheral, literary kinds. Recognized *non*literary kinds of writing include history writing, theological writing, anthropological writing, and such other writing traditions as we associate with mathematics, physics, chemistry, geology, sociology, psychology, and the other physical and behavioral sciences. Gibbon's *Decline and Fall of the Roman Empire* is recognized by historians as history, by critics as literature. Locke's *Essay Concerning Human Understanding* and Edwards's *Freedom of the Will* are recognized by critics as literature even though they originally appeared within the traditions of philosophy and theology. On the other hand, C. S. Peirce's papers in pragmatism and the writings of Albert Einstein and Max Planck, to stop just there, are in the philosophical and scientific traditions but not recognized yet as literature. And I submit that it is not something Gibbon's book possesses which has made it acceptable as literature to critics but rather something it lacks.

If a book is thought admirable by critics and is in a nonliterary kind it will be adopted into literature when it is felt to have lost a certain status in its own kind. If an historical work is regarded by historians of our own time as either bad or obsolete *as history* and critics find it deeply admirable for any of the reasons they find Tolstoy's *Anna Karenina* admirable, and Dante's *Divine Comedy* and Sheridan's *She Stoops to Conquer* and so forth, then they will begin to think of it as literature. It is apparently only nonliterary books with this status that become, in Graham Hough's phrase, "literature by special merit." [5]

Gibbon's *Decline and Fall of the Roman Empire* will serve to illustrate the point. Here is George Sherburn on the appeal of the book to the critic:

> The art of Gibbon is nowhere more noticeable than in his manner of expression. This is marked by a clear flow of narrative expressed in diction of unvarying nobility. Like a true neo-classicist he shuns "low" everyday words: a physically small man himself, he compensates with a pompous style of rhythmic sonority, definitely "noble Roman." It is obvious that he frequently writes as he does merely for the sake of the sound. Conscious effort here succeeds: the sound is always musical, and the pomp has true majesty. . . . In general the style, vivid in description and fluid in narration, enlarges and elevates the mind of the reader in spite of a chill formality.[6]

And yet the book no longer has the status it once had as history. It is not *bad* history: only the most intransigently dogmatic Christian would claim that. It is obsolete as history. What does this mean? Only that historians no longer feel it is the best treatment of its subject now available; only that they feel that if one wanted to get the most accurate possible conception of the fall of the Roman empire one should turn first to other essays, monographs, and books and only afterward to Gibbon. A bad history would be something else. If, say, all histories written on that subject since Gibbon were to be lost, it is to Gibbon that we would turn once more; if we felt it were bad history we would not turn to it even then for historical information. All those many origins-myths anthropologists have collected have almost no merit at all with us as history: they are bad history, though many are admirable for other reasons, like Gibbon's book.

Of course, for the critic, it really is not important whether the historian rates a book obsolete or bad so long as he feels it is at least obsolete. What is important to the critic, naturally, is its possession of a marked ability to "refine perception and discrimination" or to "develop the imagination" or to "offer an ideal for human life" and so forth. If it seems to him to do these things to competent readers, then he happily admits it into his understanding of literature.

Here, then, are the two major parts of fiction by value. The word fiction is not often used to cover the parts in the outer structure; and yet the word is most often used within the limits of fiction by value, and it seems a safe guess that its extensions into the outer area will become more and more common. Under the impact of pragmatism and the fictionist philosophers, the scientist's notion of the truth has changed rapidly. Here is a statement that scientists and historians are coming to feel almost commonplace. Wilbur Sanders begins by reminding us of the attitudes scientists and historians had a century ago

> when Leopold von Ranke's innocent remark that the task of the historian was "simply to show how it really was" could be taken for a profound truth. But both science and the philosophy of history have undergone marked changes since then. We now know—or think

we know—that a law is not *in nature*, waiting to be discovered, that facts will lie inert for ever if the breath of an hypothesis does not resurrect them, and that the best of our systematic knowledge of the world is no more than a mental construct, an internally consistent and pragmatically verified model which enables man to establish a kind of intellectual suzerainty over certain tracts of his environment.

Now it is as true of history as of physics that our formulations do not describe *what is*, but our own state of mind while intelligently contemplating what is.[7]

As the critic comes increasingly to think the writings of Planck and Einstein and Darwin human constructs rather than mere copies of patterns humans find in nature, the distinction between, say, the novel and the scientific paper will be harder to see and it will become easier for the word fiction to reach beyond its customary boundaries. And, too, the critic is embattled, and it is a great convenience for him to be able to claim that such novels as Melville's *Moby-Dick* and Sterne's *Tristram Shandy* and Cervantes's *Don Quixote* are members in good standing of a group that includes the work of Spinoza and Charles Darwin and Albert Einstein and Georg Riemann. These last works are given great honor in quarters that do not honor literature equally: the critic can be expected to argue that it is inventiveness of a high order that makes the work of the best scientists and philosophers most deserving of admiration and to then suggest that this same kind of inventiveness is seen even more evidently in the greatest of the novels and plays and verse that have been written.

We have now examined the two major parts of fifv, and the nine minor parts into which fifv is divided. We found a core-meaning, 'great novels,' for the word fiction, and we have identified the two interlocking nests of meanings which have that core-meaning at their single center. Later, I shall suggest that everything indicates that the word poetry has meanings attached to it which have a parallel structure, but I shall turn now to the conception of fiction as referring to genres rather than to texts.

5

Fiction as Genres

As I suggested at the very beginning of this essay, there are two radically dissimilar strategies in using the word fiction. In using the word I may have in mind a group of books: Stapledon's novel, *The Last and First Men,* and Wallace Stevens's "Sunday Morning" and Robert Burton's *Anatomy of Melancholy* and however many more you like. It is this strategy that has drawn all our attention up to this point. But I may also use the word and have in mind not the texts themselves but the traditions which produced them: perhaps I think of fiction as referring to the traditions of the autobiographical novel and the reflective poem and Menippean satire and the love lyric.

There are more courses taught in American universities with the titles The British Novel and The Modern Novel and The History of the English Novel than there are with the titles British Novels, Modern Novels, English Novels in Historical Sequence. The differences are significant: the man who designs a course he feels should be called The British Novel has a different conception of his material than the man who calls his course British Novels; the one is thinking in terms of individual books, the other in terms of genres. And it is arguable that the commonest reference of the word fiction is to genres. Most book titles critics produce suggest that, at any rate:

consider such titles as *The American Novel Today* and *Fiction Fights the Civil War* and *The Advance of the English Novel* and *The Rise of the Novel* and *An Introduction to the English Novel*. Such course and book titles suggest their authors have in mind an entity which is neither a single text nor a group of texts but rather a "genre," a "mode," a "kind," a "tradition." I shall use the word *genre*.

It is very difficult to say with any precision what a genre is. Critics are agreed genres exist, but they get very vague when one asks for operational definitions. Here is one of the more helpful attempts to explain.

> A genre is an extended convention or set of conventions working together to establish the formal nature of a whole work and to distinguish it as a particular kind of literary work. For example, an ode is formally the conflux of several conventions concerning stanzaic patterns, tone, metrics, and rhyme. There must also be a characteristic theme.[1]

This is a good beginning, but one quickly learns that further distinctions and admissions must be made if one is to capture precisely what it is critics are talking about when they use the word genre itself or when they speak of, say, poetry as distinct from poems, of the novel as distinct from novels. Is the novel a genre? If it is, what is the autobiographical novel? Is it a genre itself or is it a subgenre? Is it a subgenre of the novel, or is it a subgenre of the autobiography? And if it is also comic, what then?

A genre is a pattern. When a writer decides to make a book in a genre, he treats that pattern as an imperative. It becomes for him a system of dos and don'ts, and I think that genres are therefore most usefully described as systems of rules governing behavior. If I want to write a short story, I must follow certain rules or what I write will be something else. I must write prose, for instance, and I must complete the thing in under, say, fifty thousand words, and I must make it fiction by intention. Genres exist in people's brains as dispositions to certain kinds of patterned behavior.

But set that question of the fundamental character of the genre aside. Whatever it may finally prove to be and however we may wish to describe it, we can all agree that there are crucial kinds of distinctions a) between any given set of utterances in English and the English language itself and b) between any three or four football games and the game of football itself and c) between the pastoral elegies written by John Milton and Thomas Gray and Matthew Arnold and the tradition of the pastoral elegy itself. The English language and the game of football and the pastoral elegy are objects, too, and distinct from the objects—the specific utterances, the specific games, the specific poems—through which we learn of them. And one may prefer English to French, football to basketball, the pastoral elegy to the topographical poem; one may feel that one of those patterns in each pair has significantly greater potential for producing objects that will bring us delight and wisdom. When we feel such preferences we are thinking in terms of genres.

When F. R. Leavis advanced his choice of the best novelists who had written in English—Jane Austen, George Eliot, Henry James, Joseph Conrad, and D. H. Lawrence—he was saying something more than that their novels were among the best ever written in English. He was saying that as different as those novels are—to the sophomore the novels of James and Conrad are worlds apart—they should nevertheless be recognized as being all within a single, very fragile, very difficult genre. (He called it *the great tradition*, of course.) As interested as he was in those novels, he felt even more urgently the need to tell readers and writers that they have been ignoring a genre of immense literary potential. His book, *The Great Tradition*, is a good example of literary criticism focused essentially on a genre.

How many literary genres are there? No one knows, and we have yet to find a system of taxonomy which will allow us to make rational inventories. How many classes of genres may the word fiction be used to refer to? But we can answer *that* question: there are nine. We have already determined that.

The core meaning of the word fiction is that smallest class of books we are calling great novels. This includes those novels critics think worthy of deep admiration, those short stories and short novels and prose fiction-by-intention plays: George Eliot's *Silas Marner* and Isaac Babel's "The Sin of Jesus" and Melville's *Benito Cereno* and George Bernard Shaw's *Heartbreak House*. But *Silas Marner* may be thought of either as an object—a book—with its own special potentialities or as a representative of the genre of the novel; and as we have seen, the genre of the novel is a thing which has its own special potentialities, not all of them realized in any single novel—not even in so good a novel as *Silas Marner*. And *Silas Marner* represents not only the genre of the novel but the genre of the "great," or "serious," novel. Any of the Tom Swift novels would represent the genre of the novel as well as *Silas Marner*, but critics feel that the serious novel is different formally as well as evaluatively from trivial novels even though they have not yet been able to explain to their own satisfaction precisely what that formal difference is. And critics feel that "The Sin of Jesus" represents the genre of the serious short story, that *Benito Cereno* represents the genre of the serious short novel, that *Heartbreak House* represents the genre of the serious play. Our class great novels, then, includes works which 1) are admirable in themselves and 2) represent genres which are themselves felt to be admirable.

When this condition obtains, it is of course very easy for someone to shift from thinking of those books as objects to thinking of them as representatives and then to shift to thinking of those genres of which they are representatives. The result is that such phrases as great novels and novels and fiction by intention and great books and the five other labels we have been using will always be perfectly ambiguous to literary critics. The term novels can refer at one moment to a group of books and at another to a group of genres.

The point is crucial. Any specific set of books—to turn from words now to specific books—a critic has in his attention at any moment may "mean" either of two things to him:

1. They might seem to him representative of a much larger group of books which includes those books and others significantly like them. If I cite *Moby-Dick* and *Tom Jones* and *Don Quixote* illustratively, I may intend you to understand and bring to mind a large number of novels of equal quality—those novels I mention but also *Emma* and *The Brothers Karamazov* and *Middlemarch* and scores of others.

2. They might also seem to him representative of a group of genres which includes the genres which produced these books but also several other genres significantly like them. If I cite *Moby-Dick* and *Tom Jones* and *Don Quixote* illustratively, I may at that moment intend for you to bring to mind a certain set of writing traditions, all those we associate with the serious novel —the metaphysical romance, say, and the comic prose epic but also the experimental novel and the novel of manners.

And so that rather odd nest of meanings I have been calling fifv has a perfectly parallel nesting of meanings existing right alongside it. I shall continue to use the label fifv and shall mean the combination of both of these constructs, but for the moment let us distinguish between them by speaking of *fifv-t* and of *fifv-g*. Fifv-t is a nesting of meanings in which each meaning is a group of texts, or books. Fifv-g is a nesting of meanings in which each meaning is a group of book-producing genres. Fifv-g parallels fifv-t in every respect, and the diagram we drew of it would be simply a copy of the one we drew for fifv-t. That diagram would be a rather simple capital T with each of the two major rectangles forming the letter being a nesting of rectangles. Each of those two rectangles would be a set of six rectangles nested one inside another, and the two would share their central nesting of three rectangles.

When the word fiction is used to refer only to genres, it apparently is limited in just the way it is when used to refer to texts. In its narrowest meaning it refers to those genres which are represented by the books in great novels. It may be used to refer to other genres as well, but it will always refer to these genres too. Its largest fiction-by-value usage will be to those genres represented by all the books found in great books. Its largest fiction-by-intention usage will be to those genres represented by all the books found in fiction by intention.

The word fiction can refer to any of the nine parts of fifv-t, and it can also refer to any of the nine parts of fifv-g. It can shift within fifv-t from a fiction-by-intention orientation to a fiction-by-value orientation through a rather simple contraction to its core meaning, for instance, and an immediately subsequent expansion into a larger fiction-by-value meaning. But the word can shift from a text meaning to a genre meaning even more quickly. For each of the nine meanings in fifv-t is in immediate proximity to its parallel meaning in fifv-g. I can be speaking of fiction as simply 'novels' in the text meaning of that word and then shift to thinking of those individual novels as representative of the genres of the novel and when I have done this I have left fifv-t and entered fifv-g.

And so we must say that the word fiction has at least eighteen different meanings for the literary critic, that those eighteen meanings are intimately interconnected, and that all are in good standing in critical discourse. And this is why critical discourse employing the word fiction is sometimes so baffling and yet always, somehow, familiar; and I think it is also one of the reasons why it takes us so long to become sophisticated as critics.

Our intricate class fifv has a kind of antimatter universe existing right beside it and matching it in every detail—a universe the critic can enter and leave almost without knowing he is doing that. How are we to keep the two fifvs (fifv-t and fifv-g) clear in our discourse? It would be easy enough to do that. I might introduce a set of labels that would have both a *great novels-t* and a *great novels-g* or perhaps a ʻ*great novels*ʻ and a ʻ*great novels*ʻ or simply employ some form of capitalization to indicate the differences. I am not going to do that. I shall simply have my label great novels refer ambiguously to the two different classes. Anyone who finds it necessary to devise a terminology which keeps the difference plainly before us can always invent as sophisticated or simple a system as suits his purpose.

6

The Word Fiction as an Institution

The word fiction is epiphenomenal to critical behavior. In one sense it is misleading to say that the word has meanings; it is more useful to say that certain meanings have this word. In the brain of the literary critic is a unique set of distinctions which combine to form an immensely complicated system of categories; those categories constitute a grid which his mind superimposes on the various books and genres he encounters; and he uses the word fiction as a device for evoking in his own mind and in the minds of other critics some one or another of those categories.

The word fiction is an object, then, and it is at any given time used in that one of certain limited ways which is most useful to the critic's immediate purpose—to help him smite his enemy, say, or to help him strengthen a communion of mutual minds or to help him express his responses to a book. The word does have those eighteen meanings I have described, and those meanings are interrelated in that surprisingly simple/complex way. But if the word fiction itself were at this moment to disappear from the mind of every critic, another word would soon be slipping into the place it now occupies and that same strange complex of meanings would be evoked again.

Let us consider that complex of meanings once more

before we go on to other matters. The diagram we drew of it became absurdly complicated all of a sudden. We began with two plain rectangles forming a simple capital *T*, but now we have a second set of rectangles forming a second capital *T* right next to the first. And each of the two sets of two rectangles is subdivided into no fewer than nine rectangles. Further, the two *T*s are very closely related: we might even say they intersect, for each book critics discuss has a role to play in both *T*s. Each meaning has something in common with each of the other seventeen meanings, and it is a very simple trick to change the word fiction's meaning from any one of them to any other. But this model, however illuminating, is essentially static, and a proper description of the use of the word fiction would suggest it is dynamic.

Criticism is a way—a bundle of ways—of behaving. If a man wants his behavior to look like that of a critic, he must follow the rules critics (unconsciously) follow. Suppose one were to approach the problem in that way. Suppose one were to ask oneself what the rules are that govern the deployment of the word fiction in criticism. Here are three to begin with:

RULE 1. *Always so use the word fiction that it refers either to one or more texts or to one or more genres.*

RULE 2. *Always so use the word that any books or genres it refers to are within the class fifv.*

RULE 3. *Always have the word's meaning include the sense 'great novels.'*

Of course, in order to follow these rules one must know what the terms fifv and great novels mean, but we would provide a glossary to accompany our rules. Here are some more rules:

RULE 4. *Use the word most frequently in the sense 'great fiction by intention' or in the sense 'great prose fiction by intention' or in the sense 'great novels.'*

RULE 5. *On all other occasions use the word to refer*

exclusively to some part of fiction by value or to refer exclusively to some part of fiction by intention.

We want that last rule so our would-be critic will not combine the formal class 'novels,' say, with the evaluative class 'great books' in his use of the word. Having prevented that, we can now become more specific.

RULE 6. *When using the word with honorific overtones* (i.e., to refer to fiction by value) *always have it mean either 'great books' or only 'great literature' or only 'great imaginative literature.'*

RULE 7. *When using the word with purely formal overtones* (i.e., to refer to fiction by intention) *always have it mean 'fiction by intention' or only 'prose fiction by intention' or only 'novels.'*

If I knew enough I would add rules that guaranteed the would-be critic would use the word with precisely the frequency of distribution that bona fide critics are now using it. Here are three rules it seems safe to add:

RULE 8. *Use the word most often to mean merely 'great novels.'*

RULE 9. *Use the word least often to mean 'great books.'*

RULE 10. *Use the word more often in an honorific than in a purely formal sense.*

One of the important features of the set of rules I wrote would be that it did not include a rule that forbade the shifting of the meaning of the word in, say, mid-sentence. Quite the contrary: our rules should tell our would-be critic precisely how to do this. Here is the kind of rule we would need:

RULE 11. *To change between a text meaning and a genre meaning, change your attitude toward the books specifically under discussion: switch between thinking of them as objects representing a class of books and as objects representing a class of book-producing activities.*

And we would want to tell him how to get from one axis of fifv to another.

RULE 12. *To change the orientation of the word be-*

*tween fiction by intention and fiction by value, first con-
tract the word's sense to 'great novels' and then expand
its meaning to the desired extension along the new axis.*

What is one to say of an intellectual discipline whose
rules of conduct encourage this shiftiness of usage? The
philosopher and the scientist are half horrified and half
amused. It is axiomatic that a group's terminology must
be firmly reliable if its members are to work effectively
together. As I remarked earlier, one wonders whether
critics do understand one another when they speak.

In fact, they very often do not understand each other.
At one point I may be using the word fiction to refer to
a group of genres when you are using it to refer to a
group of texts. Since we are citing the same books (you
are interested in them for themselves, I am interested in
them only because they represent certain writing traditions), we are never quite certain we do *not* understand
one another and never quite certain we *do*. Or if we both
have books in our minds at that moment, perhaps I am
giving the word a fiction-by-value orientation and you are
giving it a fiction-by-intention orientation: I mean 'great
literature' and you mean 'novels.' Some of the books we
would cite are the same—both uses include the submean-
ing 'great novels'—and again we are not certain we do not
understand one another. There are eighteen senses in
which you can be using the word and there are seventeen
other senses in which I can be using it differently; there
are thus 18 × 17 different ways in which we can be at
variance on the meaning of the word fiction and only
18 × 1 ways in which we can be in total agreement.
Even if we take into account the fact that some uses are
more common than others and thus that some kinds of
disagreement are fairly rare, it still seems probable that
it is *uncommon* for a critic to use the word fiction and
for his readers to understand precisely what he means at
that moment.

Add to these difficulties another we have barely

touched on: critics do not always agree as to which books belong in which classes. I think B. Traven's *Bridge in the Jungle* is a great book, but few of my friends have ever heard of it; I think Thomas Hardy's *Tess of the D'Urbervilles* is a bore, but most readers I respect think it is a great novel. Throw these differences in with the others, and the possibilities for miscomprehension are multiplied. One critic cites Bunyan's *Pilgrim's Progress* as fiction and a second critic agrees. But the first is citing it because he thinks it is a great novel: it is prose, it is a narrative, it is a great book, and it is—he feels—fiction by intention. The second is citing it as fiction but is confident it is not fiction by intention; he is citing it because it is one of those books which have become great literature through adoption from a nonliterary tradition—in this case, popular theology.

In another sense, critics do understand one another, of course. There are limits to the meanings they give the word and those limits are sensed, and the meanings are closely connected with one another. Still, an atmosphere in which a central term may shift in meaning several times within a few paragraphs of exposition is not one to encourage high-level theorizing. Methodologists are concerned about this, but it is plain that practicing critics do not care. If they did care, they would themselves reduce the plurisignification and meaning-shifting they seem almost to glory in.

The most powerful descriptions of literary criticism are institutional, not cognitive. Literary criticism is a communion of people behaving, while in communion, in certain characteristic ways. Criticism is not a communal effort to determine what literature is, though critics tell themselves it is. It is a talking together about literature, and literature derives much of its importance to critics just because it gives a justification for that talking together. That talking together is, in fact, a complex of activities, not all of them verbal; and one tiny part of that complex of activities is this institutionalized using of the word fiction. The fact that critics do not care that the word shifts in meaning is one clear indication that criticism is a communion primarily and only afterward the investigation of literature it tells itself it is. Consider some of the advantages to literary criticism of these rules we have examined.

First, plurisignification of the kind we see in the word fiction actually makes the sensation of human communion more available to individual critics. If there is something about my mind that—at least temporarily—compels me to think in terms of 'great books' and there is something about your mind that has it thinking at that moment in terms of 'novels,' we have little reason to engage in a communion of minds. But if the rules for criticism permit us to use the word fiction for both these meanings and the rules identify for us a certain group of books—the great novels—which are in both our minds, then at least an illusion of common purpose is created and that agreeable sensation of being in the company of another mind thinking as you do is provided.

Second, the literary critic has been feeling embattled for a long time and these rules encourage him to feel dignity and pride even when he is being depreciated. It is plain to him that the scientist and the medical doctor and the inventive engineer is getting a kind of honor which is still denied him. The rules we have examined permit him to link himself to the most honored of all today's activities and objects. The noncritic may associate him with novels generally and verse—the good as well as the bad, of course, but the bad too—and he himself does tend to feel that what makes him unusual is the fact that he will nominate as part of great books certain works in verse and certain plays and certain works of prose fiction by intention. The individual critic who happens to feel unconsciously convinced that the work of the scientists is finally more important to the human race than his own work has a system which encourages him to find that his own interests are merely special cases of the scientist's interests. As we have seen, if the noncritic should subtly depreciate the work of the critic, the critic can show that what interests him is in the same class as the things the noncritic most admires.

And finally it is simply the case that not all minds like discourse to have clear, hard outlines. The very change-ableness of meaning in another critic's speech has its own attractions. Critics are acutely sensitive, through native ability and education, to semantic overtones and like to expose their minds to speech with immensely complex semantic burdens. Their own speech reflects this, I think, and they find the very plain style in critical essays disappointing in its meagerness. Though I think the survival value of rules which encourage changes in meaning ought not to be underestimated, perhaps it is finally this preference for complex speech which is the most important of the three reasons why critics are in no special haste to change their ways.

7

Some Further Queries

The theories I have presented do have implications. They give us a new basis for considering once again some very old questions: 1) Can a novel tell the truth? 2) Can a novel tell a lie? 3) What is nonfiction? They also give us an insight into other terms critics use: 4) When is something poetry? And, finally, they raise a question of more than literary significance: 5) What roles does fiction by intention play?

Can a novel tell the truth? It is a commonplace in aesthetics and criticism—though not universally accepted even there—that a novelist cannot "affirm" and therefore cannot "lie." Here is the best-known statement of that position; it appears in Sir Philip Sidney's *Apology for Poetry*.

> Now, for the poet, he nothing affirms, and therefore never lieth. For, as I take it, to lie is to affirm that to be true which is false; so as the other artists, and especially the historians, affirming many things, can, in the cloudy knowledge of mankind, hardly escape from many lies. But the poet (as I said before) never affirmeth.

The context in which these sentences occur makes it quite plain that Sidney is speaking of the writer of fiction by intention rather than the writer of verse, and it is plain enough, too, that the verb *lie* should be understood to mean simply 'make an error.' The historian, Sidney said, tries to say things about reality and—man being what he is—cannot escape making many mistakes, but the writer of fiction by intention "has knowingly made his book factually untrue but has also warned his reader he has done this" and therefore cannot make mistakes about reality. And I want to raise these three questions: Does the writer of fiction by intention "affirm"? Can his book be in error about reality? And can he be guilty of having told deliberate untruths about reality? Sidney really did not ask this last question, but I shall ask it anyway.

Whatever else it may be, it is certainly historically inaccurate for any critic to claim that writers do not affirm in their novels. Here is Joseph Conrad:

> Art itself may be defined as a single-minded attempt to render the highest kind of justice to the visible universe, by bringing to light the truth, manifold and one, underlying its every aspect. It is an attempt to find in its forms, in its colours, in its light, in its shadows, in the aspects of matter, and in the facts of life what of each is fundamental, what is enduring and essential—their one illuminating and convincing quality—the very truth of their existence.[1]

Clearly, Conrad was trying to affirm something in his novels, and so were, and are, hundreds of other writers of fiction by intention. It is true that a certain frame of facts within each of his novels was his own invention and that he expected his readers to recognize this, but he was affirming as truth a heavy propositional burden (and much natural description, too) that was being carried by that fiction-by-intention frame.

There is a person who assures us that a sentence with a double negative must be positive in meaning—but that clearly ain't not the case. He himself recognizes that the designer of the double negative means the sentence to be negative: he knows instantly that the sentence is "wrong," and how could he know that if he took the sentence to say a positive thing? The people who tell us —as Sidney did—that a work of fiction by intention cannot affirm are treating the work as though it had been written according to the conventions of mathematics. If I multiply a minus quantity by a minus quantity, I get a plus quantity in mathematics; but no god has ever declared that natural human languages must be so superbly nonredundant as mathematics, and none of them are. And novel-writing is not an activity which has zero redundancy as its goal either. Even though the novelist declares that he is the inventor of the story he will tell us, we all know enough to suspect that he really wants us to distinguish between the parts he invented and the other parts in which he is giving what he feels he observed.

In practice, critics and other readers have always recognized this. Eric Auerbach remarks of Zola that "almost every line he wrote showed that all this was meant in the highest degree seriously and morally, that the sum total of it was not a pastime or an artistic parlor game but the true portrait of contemporary society as he— Zola—saw it and as the public was being urged in his works to see it too." [2] And here is Irving Howe, one of the best known of contemporary American literary critics:

> In *The Assistant* Bernard Malamud has written a somber story about a Jewish family during the Depression years, yet it soon becomes clear that one of his impelling motives is a wish to recapture intensities of feeling we have apparently lost but take to be characteristic of an earlier decade. Herbert Gold's

The Man Who Was Not With It is an account of marginal figures in a circus as they teeter on the edge of *lumpen* life; but soon one realizes that he means his story to indicate possibilities for personal survival in a world increasingly compressed.

In the comments that follow—too long to be given here—Howe makes it quite clear that he feels J. D. Salinger is asserting in *The Catcher in the Rye*, that Nelson Algren is asserting in *A Walk on the Wild Side*, that Wright Morris is asserting in *The Field of Vision*, and that Saul Bellow is asserting in *The Adventures of Augie March* and *Henderson the Rain King*.[3] It would not be difficult, it would be merely tedious, to cite a hundred parallel comments on the assertions found in works of fiction, and all from men accepted as literary critics of merit.

Novelists and other writers of fiction by intention do claim that they are asserting, and critics recognize this and even take the trouble to explain to the baffled reader what it is each writer *is* asserting. And if a man does assert something, he may be mistaken in what he asserts. It is true that the novelist is not asserting that his book is factually true as a whole, but I think more often than not he is claiming that his text is factually true in part and propositionally true in general. And often, in these cases, he is lying in the sense that Sidney used the word: he is asserting to be true what is actually not true. Would any of us seriously suggest that George Orwell's 1984 is not a novel? that Orwell was not asserting in it something he believed true? and have not many of us thought it true and many of us thought it false?

Can a novel tell a lie? This is a much more interesting question than the question of whether a novelist (or any other writer of fiction by intention) can assert a truth. If a man can assert a truth, he can assert a falsehood;

and it should take no special array of argument to demonstrate—my previous arguments having been granted—that a man can write a novel which tells a lie.

Suppose I were to write one of those academic novels English teachers are always writing. I have taught in several universities and might write a novel about one of them. I would invent new names for the school and for my former colleagues, but they would know instantly that I was talking about them. I suppose I would avoid presenting any of my colleagues precisely as he appeared to me: I would throw one or two wholly invented characters among them, and the others I would form by combining characteristics that are separated in reality. There must be dozens upon dozens of that kind of novel around—many of them in print.

Now consider the reception that novel of mine might receive from the critics I was actually writing about. They might decide that the impression I give of the school and its faculty is substantially accurate. They might feel the impression was inaccurate but honestly mistaken: they would be questioning my judgment, not my sincerity. Or—and this may even be most likely—they might feel that the impression I give of them is not only false but dishonest. I may be offering a grandiose portrait of the school—I want to be rehired, perhaps. Or I may be offering a humiliating portrait—a consciously spiteful distortion of what I know to be the truth. And in this last case, those critics would not hesitate to call me a liar. They would not stop to assure themselves that a "poet" never "affirms" and therefore never "lies." [4]

In practice, critics are always saying that one can write a novel which is a lie. But if a work of fiction by intention may sometimes be a lie, then the relations that obtain between lies and fiction by intention ought to be looked at rather closely in a book offering a theory of fiction. Lying is misrepresentation. There are many texts which are neither true nor false (a prayer, for instance, or a legal contract); but many texts can be declared to be the one or the other. Lying is the presenting of a false text as true or a true text as false. More accurately: it is the presentation of a text one *thinks* false as true, or of a text one thinks true as false—one can be unsuccessful at lying as at anything else.

Probably the most frequent form of the lie is the telling of something one thinks false as though one thought it true, but this is not the only form the lie takes. The precisely opposite kind of lie is the inverse lie, and it, too, is common; in this case, a truthful statement is made in such a manner as to persuade one to disbelieve it. They pop up fairly often in detective stories; for instance, in Raymond Chandler's "Bay City Blues" the killer attempts to divert suspicion from himself by saying, as though it were unthinkable, "Sure. I killed her." And this kind of lie is found elsewhere: in order to seem innocent, Moliere's Tartuffe quite accurately describes himself as a villain. One version of the inverse lie is found in stage plays: one of the characters in the play comments to the effect that everything happening is so strange that he feels "like a character in a play." Tom Pinch in chapter 50 of Dickens's *Martin Chuzzlewit* patiently explains to his sister that he is not "a character in a book."

But these are quite simple types of the lie, and a system built on such plain distinctions will not cope with the problem presented by the dishonest novel. Apparently we must begin by recognizing at least those two kinds of truth I have already referred to: factual truth and propositional truth. And we must recognize also that a text may be true in neither or either or both of these ways. This gives us four categories:

1. factually true and propositionally true;
2. factually false and propositionally false;

3. factually true but propositionally false; and
4. factually false but propositionally true.

If somcone identifies his book as one of these four types but presents it as any one of the other types, he is lying. A very simple computation will show that this system of distinctions identifies twelve kinds of lies for us: a text in any one of the four categories may be presented as though it belonged to any one of the remaining three categories. The system is not much of an improvement over the one that recognizes only true texts and false texts and has them represented as their opposites, but we do not need any very complicated system to make the general point that there is no great mystery about the novelist's being accused of lying every now and then. In accusing him of lying we are saying that he has written a book which he knows is of the second of these four types—it is factually and propositionally false—but has presented it to his readers as though it were of the fourth type—only factually and not propositionally false.

I will not claim very much for this system I have devised; it comes nowhere near covering all the difficulties we encounter when investigating the connections between writing lies and writing fiction by intention. For one thing, a text may seem to us to be factually part true and part false and propositionally part true and part false, and this system does not recognize that. It is also defective in that it does not even consider what is now being called *presentational truth,* which is important to some critics. Echoic verse may be said to offer the presentational truth to what it describes in that the verse itself has some of the qualities of the thing it describes. A text which is neither factually nor propositionally true may be presentationally true, I suppose, but this system does not admit this. And finally there seem to be some erratic uses of the word *lie* which the system does not recognize. For one example, sometimes a novelist is accused of being dishonest when he presents what the reader thinks is too sentimental or too noble or even too grim a view of reality. The claim, in this case, is not that the writer is not presenting what he sees but that he is guilty of not having exercised enough care in his examination of reality. This we might call *negligent dishonesty*, or *negligent lying*, on an analogy with the phrase *negligent homicide* (a term used when a man has been held to be culpable for killing a person even though he did not intend to kill). An overpatriotic book may angrily be branded a lie in this sense (as were the motion pictures John Wayne made during the Vietnam war), and I think Harriet Beecher Stowe's *Uncle Tom's Cabin* was called a lie in this sense by Southern newspaper critics of its time.

My system is defective in these ways and no doubt in other respects as well. Still, it does indicate that the naïve reader or critic who claims certain novels are dishonest is sometimes not quite so naïve as we theoreticians who have assured him that fiction by intention cannot lie—in either sense of the word—because it cannot assert.

What is nonfiction? The word *nonfiction* offers its own problems in definition, and I have tried to get along without using it while discussing the word fiction. It is ambiguous too, but in its own way. Critics use the word nonfiction to refer at any given moment to either of two classes of books or genres. Sometimes it means 'not-fiction,' which is whatever the word fiction does not mean at that moment. Sometimes it means 'antifiction,' which is only that part of not-fiction which is felt to be the *rival* of whatever fiction refers to at that moment.

The meaning 'not-fiction' need not delay us. If at one moment the word fiction refers to the books which critics identify as great novels, then nonfiction in the sense 'not-fiction' refers to all other books. It then refers both to never-fiction (all the books which are never named fiction by critics) but also to those books sometimes named fiction but which are not included in the sense of the word at that moment. Clearly it is useful for critics to have a word which plays this role.

But the pejorative sense of nonfiction—'antifiction'— is more frequently evoked, I believe; and it is useful to have a word with this role, too. The difficulty lies in having a single word which plays both roles: here too the opportunities for inadvertent shifts in meaning are very great. Antifiction is the rival of fiction. If the word fiction refers to all novels in a particular discussion, then antifiction is at that time the class of those books or genres which the critic's opponent identifies as superior to novels; if the word fiction refers to all novels, then nonfiction-antifiction does not refer to any novels. But when fiction refers to great novels only, then antifiction is usually sensed as certain novels—those which are only popular, not admirable. I submit that antifiction is the class of books or genres which threatens fiction either by winning the admiration of people who might otherwise admire fiction or by winning their attention.

One very common use of nonfiction-antifiction is to refer to a class that is currently felt to rival all of fiction by intention. I propose that we call this class *mimiture*; we ought to have a name that identifies it very explicitly. When the word mimiture refers to genres, it is referring to the writing traditions which would have men produce texts that are *only* true; when it refers to texts, it is referring to the books produced in those traditions. All of the books historians and scientists and philosophers are writing today are the result of their attempts to produce books that are only true. Fiction by intention in all its forms directs its writers to produce texts that may be true in the most profound senses of the word but which are not *only* true: they are always supposed to have at least a factual frame which is untrue. If I told a novelist that parts of his book are untrue, he would reply, "Of course!" But if I were to tell a scientist that parts of his essay are untrue, he would become upset; he is writing in the tradition of mimiture.

Mimiture and fiction by intention do not divide all books among them. There are many texts which belong to neither class: curses, prescriptions, oaths of allegiance, and so forth. But the two general traditions I have labeled fiction by intention and mimiture are important, and it is perfectly plain that people who are not literary critics have more faith in the potential of mimiture than they do in fiction by intention. When they think of the traditions of mimiture they think of achievement and satisfaction and instruction and discovery; when they think of the traditions in fiction by intention they think of entertainment. It is an inaccurate characterization of fiction by intention, but it is the one that obtains among noncritics.

To sum up: Nonfiction takes its meaning by reference to the meaning of fiction at any moment, and it may have either of two different kinds of meaning. It may refer to what would more accurately be called not-fiction or it may refer to what may be called antifiction. The antifiction meaning of nonfiction is very frequently 'mimiture.'

There is much more to be said about all this than that, obviously, and there are some curious relations to investigate: I suspect, for instance, that fiction by intention and mimiture may be coeval in Western culture: that the distinction between the two has not been clear for us until about the eighteenth century and—perhaps because of?—the rise of science. But there are many other categories to be identified and many strange relations among the various meanings of such terms as nonfiction and fraud and fiction.

I suggest that any interested person might find it useful, as I did, to construct a certain chart. The chart becomes rather complicated—it has 128 categories—but it is constructed on very simple principles. Of each book, one asks the following six yes/no questions:

1. Does the writer believe his book is factually true?
2. Does he believe it is propositionally true?
3. Does he want his readers to believe it is factually true?
4. Does he want them to believe it is propositionally true?
5. Is the book really factually true?
6. Is it really propositionally true?

Since the first question may be answered with either a yes or a no and the second question can be given either of these two answers and each of the other questions also, it can be seen that these six questions will generate a total of two to the sixth power, or 128, categories. (The questions are wholly inappropriate to some books, of course, but we are ignoring them.)

In an early stage of the work for this book I actually did construct such a chart. I do not think I tested every single one of those 128 categories, but my friends and I examined a good many of them and discovered that we could always imagine a text that would fit that category and could almost always *name* such a text. Thus, any text for which we would answer both the first and third questions in that list with a no would be an instance of fiction by intention however we might answer the other four questions. And any text for which we would answer the first four of these questions with a yes would be an instance of mimiture. And if we answer the first question about a text with a no and the third question with a yes we have identified a particular kind of lie; if we then proceed to answer the fifth question with a yes we have identified that lie as unsuccessful: the writer wanted to tell an untruth but inadvertently told the truth (Jean-Paul Sartre has a character doing this in his short story, "The Wall," for instance). And so forth. It also reminds us of such occasional oddities as books that are substantially true even on the literal level but are labeled *novel* by their authors, which is a rather special kind of fraud. No doubt the chart could be made even more complexly responsive to critical perceptions and be made to account for an even greater variety of books.

When is something poetry? The concept-structure behind the word poetry is more complex than the one behind fiction, but it is closely parallel. I think that is an important discovery. Each of the most central terms in critical discourse—poetry and literature and drama, for instance—expands and contracts along two axes within each of two sets of objects. I do not understand fully the intricacies of the concept-structure behind poetry, but its more obvious features are revealing.

The word poetry is used in a bewildering variety of ways, as we all know, but it does have a core meaning. Any critic who uses the word today has it refer to the class *great lyrics* at least; anyone who suggested that poetry did *not* include the greatest lyric poems written would be thought highly eccentric. One rule for the use of the word poetry in criticism, then, is that it must be given the signification 'great lyrics.' [5] And this core meaning—like the meaning 'great novels' for fiction—has two different values: it may be a reference to a set of individual poems or it may be a reference to the genres which have produced those poems.

But the word poetry at one time or another expands to mean more than just 'great lyrics.' We find people saying that in one sense poetry includes even mnemonic verse ("Thirty days hath September"), and we find them saying that Fitzgerald's novel *The Great Gatsby* is a poem, and we find them saying that Darwin's *Origin of*

Species is a poem.[6] This amounts to saying at one moment that poetry is all verse, at another that it is all great imaginative literature, and at a third that it is all great books.

It encourages us to construct a diagram closely modeled on the one we drew for the term fiction. Again we will have two plain rectangles crossing one another to form a simple capital T and we will have a parallel T right next to the first. We will call this superclass *pipv*, an acronym suggesting the phrases *poetry by intention* (which is verse) and *poetry by value* (which is a unique articulation of the class great books). One of the Ts might be called *pipv-t* and the other *pipv-g*. Each is divided into seven different classes. The word poetry never refers to anything outside the boundaries of pipv, but it never refers to all of pipv. In this, it behaves just like the word fiction. It always means one or another of the fourteen classes within pipv.

The vertical rectangle in the T is poetry by intention: this is the class for which critics already have a word—*verse*. I shall use the word verse instead of the phrase poetry by intention because it is more familiar and also less awkward to handle in a sentence. Of course the class verse overlaps with fiction by intention—Keats's "The Eve of St. Agnes" and Frost's "The Witch of Coös" belong to both classes—but neither is wholly subsumed by the other: Scott's *Old Mortality* is not verse and Pope's *Essay on Man* is not fiction by intention. The internal structure of verse may very well be more complicated than that of fiction by intention, but I shall not attempt to analyze it fully here. Let us merely identify within verse the smaller class *lyrics*; epic poems are not lyrics and verse plays are not lyrics, for instance. For the past hundred years or so, the lyric has been at the center of the critic's attention, and the word poetry is thought of first in connection with the lyric and only afterward in connection with, say, the epic. And so we have a large class, verse, with a wholly contained subclass, lyrics.

When we make the horizontal rectangle, great books, intersect the vertical rectangle, verse, the two classes we have been considering are divided. We now have the subclass great lyrics and another subclass great verse, which contains great lyrics as well as other poetry. The class poetry by intention is now divided into four classes, and each is at one time or another a meaning for the word poetry: 'great lyrics' and 'great verse' and 'lyrics' and 'verse.' Great lyrics, of course, are the works which are lyric and also deserve to be deeply admired, and the term also refers to the writing traditions which produced those works.

Poetry by value has an inner structure and an outer structure, just as fiction by value has. In fact, the outer structure of this class is precisely the same: we find three classes which also appear as meanings for the word poetry—'great books' and 'great literature' and 'great imaginative literature.' We have already discussed their characteristics in connection with the word fiction.

The inner structure is unique. We can see this if we return to our diagram. We shall insert into the rectangle which is great imaginative literature a nest of two rectangles of which the larger is great verse and the smaller great lyrics. And now we have the interlocking meanings of the word poetry. Its core meaning is 'great lyrics' but it may be expanded out along the axis of poetry by value to mean 'great verse' or 'great imaginative literature' or 'great literature' or 'great books.' Or it may be extended out along the axis of poetry by intention to mean either 'lyrics' or 'verse.' Further, the individual poems, or works, being discussed at any given moment may seem representative either of a larger class of discrete works or of a class of writing traditions—genres—which are supposed to have produced them. When a critic tells us that even mnemonic verse is poetry, he is having the word mean 'verse.' When he tells us Melville's short novel *Benito Cereno* is poetry, he is having the word mean 'great imaginative literature' at the very least. And when he tells us that the very greatest works the scientists have produced are poetry, too, then he is having it mean 'great books.'

This model is very crude. For one thing, there is increasing tendency for critics to use the word poetry in connection with distinctions between the metaphoric and the nonmetaphoric and to ignore the verse/prose distinctions, and the model does not recognize that. But it does have the merit of indicating how significant this pivoting of key terms between purely formal and purely honorific axes of meaning is to critical discourse.

What kind of model would we have if we combined the model of the concept-structure behind fiction with that of the concept-structure behind poetry and the other concept-structures behind the terms drama and literature? A skillful draftsman might make a diagram which combined all those classes and subclasses and showed their intersection with one another, but it would be immensely difficult to read. At any rate, we would have about reached the limits of usefulness for verbal and visual models of concept-structures, I think. Anyone who wants to go beyond that point will probably find that he has to turn to topological mathematics for help. The thought that someone interested in literary criticism might turn for help to mathematics is most disagreeable for critics, but I think this is not a case in which their mistrust is valid. We shall not be turning to mathematics for help in computing literary values; we shall be turning to it because it is a stockpile of models of relationships and some of those models will prove useful to us. The meaning-to-meaning relationships we work with are too complex—because *we* are too complex in our perceptions and thought—for the kinds of verbal definitions we find in literary glossaries (which are, after all, intended for the beginner) or for charts made up of simple rectangles subdividing one another. We need better ways of describing if we are going to understand ourselves better and explain ourselves adequately to others.

What role is fiction by intention playing in Western culture? This question is really outside my own competence, but certain sociologists and anthropologists and philosophers *are* competent to take it up and it is something of a disappointment to discover that they have not. The literary critic can be expected to confine himself to great fiction by intention, but someone should be asking about all fiction by intention, the trivial as well as the great. Here are some questions that intrigue me.

A friend has suggested that we do not really know how it is that a child comes to recognize that the story of Peter Rabbit is an invented story like a lie but that the man who tells that story should not be punished. How *do* children learn in our culture what fiction by intention is? How long does it take them? What status vis-à-vis reality does any text (film, picture, etc.) seem to them to have at first? Does the status of mimimure have to be taught them too?

And this question suggests some others. The man who speaks fiction by intention establishes a particular complex of relations among himself, his utterance, and his listener. Do all human cultures recognize this set of discourse relations? Is fiction by intention, like language, a thing which is natural to humans or is it one more human invention? It is so familiar a mode of discourse in the Western world that we tend to think of it as an inevitable part of human relations, I suppose, but the hypothesis that it is an invention, like the spinning wheel and the six-based number system, has great heuristic potential.

Where we know the history of an invention, whether in technology, art, thought, or custom, we almost invariably find that it has not been made independently by a number of peoples in different places and at different times but by one people in one place and at a particular moment of their history, and that it has spread, wholly or in part, from this people to other peoples. When we look into the matter further we find that there have been a limited number of centres of important cultural development and diffusion, and also that in the process of borrowing and incorporation into other cultures the diffused traits may undergo all sorts of modifications and changes. Since it can be shown that the inventions for the history of which we have reliable evidence have almost invariably diffused in this manner it is not unreasonable to suppose, when we find similar artifacts, ideas, and customs among primitive peoples in different parts of the world, that these have in the same way spread from a limited number of points of cultural advancement, even though there is no other evidence of their having done so than that contained in their similarity and their geographical distribution; especially if the traits are at all complex and are also found in association.[7]

I am sure it would be much easier to trace the invention and subsequent diffusion of the quiver or of gravestone symbolism or of a particular way of handling cattle than to trace a rhetorical pattern or a number system or this matter of fiction by intention, but surely it would be worth the effort for professional anthropologists? So far as I have been able to determine, the concept of fiction by intention as a thing that was invented by one culture and then borrowed by other cultures does not appear in the writings of anthropologists and sociologists. Professor Paul Radin seems perfectly representative of an earlier generation of anthropologists when he remarked, "Every field-worker in anthropology who has the slightest understanding of literature knows today that literary artists exist in every preliterate community, that they are recognized as such by the community, and that, moreover, fictional and semi-historical narratives are told for the sheer delight of telling them." [8] It is quite evident from the sentences I quoted earlier that the Ashanti and the Sudanese do recognize that category fiction by intention, and apparently hundreds of other cultures do too. But histories of Chinese and of Japanese literature invariably include the observation that the word we translate fiction suggests something rather different to readers in that culture than it does to us.[9] And, really, we need not go outside Western culture to find evidence that some people do not recognize that set of discourse-relations we are calling fiction by intention, for one of the first things we learn in a survey of English literature is that the Puritans during the sixteenth and seventeenth centuries did not (*could* not) distinguish between the man who wrote fiction by intention and the man who wrote an out-and-out lie. If there are subcultures even within our own culture that do not recognize that someone may be speaking fiction by intention, surely we are justified in suspecting that there may be cultures that have neither invented nor borrowed that form of discourse. I suspect that remarks like the one quoted from Professor Radin do not actually address this question. Those remarks are intended to defend "savage" cultures from the denigration they still receive in direct and indirect ways: even today, the typical humanist regards primitive peoples as less than human—they are "backward"—or as more than human—they are closer to "the primal source"—but rarely as *just* human. But it does not seem to me that it is a denigration of primitive cultures to suggest that some of them do not know the device of speaking fiction by intention.[10] It is no more a denigration to say that than it is to say that one or another of them has not invented the sonnet. And the question of invention and borrowing is not an idle one, for its answers might suggest answers to more important questions: What are the uses to which a culture puts fiction by intention? Which kinds of cultures need a device of this kind and thus exploit it to the full when they discover it? Which cultures have no use for it and remain indifferent? Which cultures—the English Puritans, for example—feel threatened by it? Why?

And even if we were never to look beyond our own Western world, there are still questions of this kind to be asked. For example, sleight-of-hand performers today suggest very clearly that what they are doing is not done through true magical powers—and yet follow this disclaimer with magical effects they refuse to explain. This is, I suppose, another form of fiction by intention. And the television personality makes it quite plain to his viewers that he is reading his lines from cards held out of camera range; this too seems related to fiction by intention. How pervasive in our own culture is this strategy? How are we using it? Why?

Notes

Introduction

1. See the structural formula of the monosyllabic word in English which is given in Benjamin Lee Whorf, *Language, Thought, and Reality* (Cambridge, Mass.: M.I.T. Press, 1956), p. 223. See also the diagram that shows "that part of an English utterance up to and including the first vowel" in Zellig S. Harris, *Structural Linguistics* (1947; rpt. Chicago: University of Chicago Press, Phoenix Books, 1951), p. 153.

2 – Fiction by Intention

1. Cited by Susan Feldman in *African Myths and Tales* (New York: Dell, 1963), p. 12. This Sudanese disclaimer sets up a paradoxical truth/untruth claim, but I suspect that the Sudanese audience also distinguishes, like the Western literary critic, between factual and propositional truth and admits of broader claims of value than just that of telling propositional truths.

2. Ian Watt remarks on the importance of "realistic particularity" in the development of the novel and on the novel-reader's hunger for circumstantial detail. See *The Rise of the Novel: Studies in Defoe, Richardson, and Fielding* (1957; rpt. Berkeley: University of California Press, 1965), pp. 15–18, 31.

3. René Wellek and Austin Warren, *Theory of Literature*, 3rd ed. (New York: Harcourt, 1956), pp. 212–13.

4. Even a sophisticated critic will forget himself on this point sometimes, however. In Northrop Frye's account of

the Egyptian tale, "The Two Brothers," he refers to one of its incidents—the one in which the god Ra places a crocodile-filled lake in the way of the pursuers of the innocent younger brother—as a part of the story in which the storyteller has given up "the external analogy to 'life'." (See *Anatomy of Criticism: Four Essays* [Princeton, N. J.: Princeton University Press, 1957], p. 135.) But this is to assume what is quite uncertain: that the Egyptian storyteller's sense of life was the same as our own. It is very difficult to maintain a continuously keen sense of what it is like to accept as simple history stories that include the kinds of events we ourselves term fantastic and mythical. Even the field anthropologist finds that difficult, apparently; see the essays cited by William Bascom in "The Forms of Folklore: Prose Narratives," *Journal of American Folklore* 78 (1965), 3–20.

5. It used to be felt that any reference to the intention of the writer was a clear indication of critical naivety. But it is quite plain that critics have always taken the writer's intention into account in at least some cases. If we did not do this, we would not be distinguishing between a parody of a writer's style and an unsuccessful imitation of it; we say some works are parodies because we feel it is evident that their writers were intentionally trying to be funny-bad. It is this kind of estimate of intention that the critic has in the back of his mind, at least, when he identifies a book as fiction by intention.

6. Monroe C. Beardsley, *Aesthetics: Problems in the Philosophy of Criticism* (New York: Harcourt, 1958), p. 442. The whole of the essay which is Beardsley's source for the story is worth reading; see Robert Wallace, "A Word of Caution to Tort-Feasors," *The Reporter*, 30 June 1955, p. 35.

Most of us are indignant when we read that a judge has forced a novelist to pay damages to a plaintiff even though it was clear the writer had not intended to refer to the plaintiff; but it would be difficult for the judge to take any other course. If some innocent person has really been damaged in his reputation by a book which brought profit to the writer, the person who has been hurt ought to be given some recompense.

7. It is instructive to compare the attitudes critics have toward Carlyle's *Sartor Resartus* and Thackeray's *Vanity Fair*. Carlyle's book has a fiction-by-intention frame carrying a huge mass of sentences the author would have presented as expressing his own deepest convictions. Thackeray's book is just the reverse: the writer speaks in his own person about the work of fiction-by-intention he is inventing. The first does have a fiction-by-intention frame, but it is not treated as a novel by critics; the second has a fiction-by-intention bulk carried by a frame which is not fiction by intention in character, but critics treat it as a novel.

8. Evert A. Duyckinck, "Melville's *Moby-Dick*; or The Whale," *New York Literary World* 9 (Nov. 22, 1851), 403–4; as reprinted in Herman Melville, *Moby-Dick*, ed. Harrison Hayford and Hershel Parker, Norton Critical Edition (New York: Norton, 1967), pp. 613–14. See also, in this connection, the essay by Walter E. Bezanson which is reprinted in that volume, esp. pp. 652–55.

9. Two readers of an earlier version of this book objected strongly to this sentence, but it seems to me unexceptionable. Suppose I were to give you the assignment of describing in words any real object you wished to choose and required that you describe it so completely that no person who examined the real object could ever find any feature in it you had not described: would you accept this challenge?

I think that what people object to in this sentence is an imagined implication that I find life richer than books, but I do not have this in mind. I believe, for instance, that any contemporary of Henry James would have gained a much finer and truer sense of the world James lived in by reading his novels than he would have gained by experiencing that world itself directly: Henry James had a mind that saw things others did not see. But surely James presented only a selection of the things he saw in that world? Surely that world was *factually* richer than his books?

10. It has been proved often enough that the police do sometimes fabricate the evidence they need to convict men they have accused of crimes, but often—not always—they have done this illegal thing in the interests of what they feel is a higher morality: they wanted to get men convicted

of crimes they felt the men really did commit. The detectives who learn that a man selling addictive drugs is too clever ever to be caught with drugs in his possession will plant drugs on him—so that what they know to be the truth will also be evident to a jury.

It is not unlikely that the infamous Protocols of Zion were fabricated by men who were lying in what they thought was the interest of truth. See John S. Curtiss, *An Appraisal of the Protocols of Zion* (New York: Columbia University Press, 1942): see especially p. 71 for the theory of one publisher of the Protocols that God may have made someone produce those Protocols *as a lie* so that mere humans would see the truth about the Jewish conspiracy.

11. As reprinted in *Literature for Composition*, ed. James R. Kreuzer and Lee Cogan (New York: Holt, Rinehart, 1965), p. 261. Such authentications are so familiar to the reader of the adventure stories written in the early part of this century—and I speak as a man who has gulped down barrels of that stuff—that they very nearly achieve the status of signals that what is to follow is *not* to be taken as factually true; but surely they started as attempts to get the reader into the world that was to be described—or, rather, to get that world into the reader's world. They were written in the hopes of deceiving readers.

12. From a notebook entry of Hardy cited in Miriam Allott, *Novelists on the Novel* (1959; rpt. New York: Columbia University Press, 1966), p. 58.

13. Quoted from *Joseph Conrad: A Personal Remembrance* in Howard E. Hugo, *Aspects of Fiction: A Handbook* (Boston: Little, Brown, 1962), p. 130.

14. *Lucian: True History and Lucius or the Ass*, trans. Paul Turner (Bloomington, Indiana: Indiana University Press, 1958), p. 4.

15. See also Beardsley, *Aesthetics*, pp. 138, 421. I strongly recommend Professor Beardsley's book to those who would like to compare the view of fiction by intention I present with those of other writers. See especially pp. 411–14, 419–23, for an account to which I am indebted but which I cannot wholly accept.

16. It is conceivable that some researcher will pursue the

notion that fiction by intention is marked by distinctive vocabulary items and distinctive sentence-structures. (I do not remember ever seeing a study predicated on this assumption, but I have heard men with a special interest in stylistics suggest this orally.) I think this kind of investigation would be a waste of time. There are other kinds of stylistic investigation that seem to me quite promising in their own ways, however. One kind that is currently intriguing critics is that represented by David Lodge's *Language of Fiction: Essays in Criticism and Verbal Analysis of the English Novel* (New York: Columbia University Press, 1966). Professor Lodge makes exploratory extensions of techniques of novel reading based on the models of lyric reading which were devised by the New Critics. It is quite different from anything I am dealing with here.

17. It is not impossible that there are enough books like those of Daniel Defoe and Mrs. Aphra Behn recognized by critics as fiction by intention so that I should have given them more attention than I have. During the late seventeenth and early eighteenth centuries there seems to have developed a new genre—a realistic romance—which, dealing with contemporary life, preceded such realistic traditions as produced the best-known novels of the eighteenth and nineteenth centuries. These books falsely presented themselves as authentic factual accounts of reality—and were thus, in the strictest interpretation, lies—but they are all accepted now by literary critics as fiction by intention. For some description of this genre and for a detailed account of the interesting devices the writers used to authenticate their inventions, see A. J. Tieje, "A Peculiar Phase of the Theory of Realism in Pre-Richardsonian Prose-Fiction," *PMLA* 28 (1913), 213–52.

The matter of Defoe's book is much more complicated than I have allowed it to appear. A good insight into the kinds of problems Defoe (and, I suppose, many of his contemporaries) faced when they were obliged to invent stories but were also persuaded that invention was dishonest is provided by Maximillian E. Novak, "Defoe's Theory of Fiction," *Studies in Philology* 16 (1964), 650–68.

18. Norman N. Holland has some observations on the same matter in "Prose and Minds: A Psychoanalytic Approach to Non-Fiction," in *The Art of Victorian Prose*, ed. George Levine and William Madden (New York: Oxford University Press, 1968), 314–37; see especially pp. 320–22 and 332–33.

I offer anyone interested in studying the precise boundary between fiction by intention and autobiography the problems presented by Mary McCarthy's *Memories of a Catholic Girlhood* (New York: Harcourt, 1957). Miss McCarthy helps the reader out by telling him quite firmly which parts definitely are fiction, which parts definitely are not fiction, and which parts may or may not be fiction—which left me more confused than I would have been without that help.

3—*Fiction by Value*

1. In this second list I am citing books critics are generally agreed are bad—bad in literary terms, at least. There is a special difficulty in citing bad books that I have never seen anyone comment on. Anyone concerned about literary values must refer to the bad as well as the good, but he encounters a curious limitation in the titles available. The books critics admire are more widely known than the ones they despise. A moment's reflection makes this seem quite natural: we do not recommend to one another the books we do not admire, and most of the bad never do get widely known.

I would like to make my list of bad books as varied as my list of good books, and I might do that—but it is pointless to list a large number of texts one or another group of critics thinks bad when most critics have never even heard of them. I am thus forced—as others have been before me—to cite those titles that are always cited. But this is dangerous as well as tiresome. The books critics think bad—Margaret Mitchell's *Gone With the Wind*, say, and Joyce Kilmer's "Trees"—have a way of coming to be regarded by another generation first with amused affection and then with growing respect. The writer then begins to look foolish. It was

no less a man than David Hume, after all, who flatly declared in *Of the Standard of Taste* that "whoever would
assert an equality of genius and elegance between . . . Bunyan and Addison would be thought to defend no less an
extravagance than if he had maintained a molehill to be as
high as Teneriffe, or a pond as extensive as the ocean." And
we tend to agree that the one had a greater genius, but in
precisely the opposite sense from the one Hume intended. I
have chosen a couple of novels and some poems that were
well known and generally regarded as bad within the past
decade.

One reminder. My lists report what critics think as a group.
I do not always share the attitudes of the group. I dislike
Charlotte Bronte's *Jane Eyre* as much, I think, as I do any
of these texts I have listed as bad, but if I had to add it to
one of the lists I would of course add it to the list of those
critics think admirable.

2. Monroe C. Beardsley, *Aesthetics: Problems in the Philosophy of Criticism* (New York: Harcourt, 1958), pp. 574–
75.

3. N. W. Pirie, "Orthodox and Unorthodox Methods of
Meeting World Food Needs," *Scientific American* 216, No.
3 (February 1967), 34.

4. How does the individual critic determine that something he does not admire nevertheless deserves his admiration, that something he does admire does not deserve it, etc.?
I go into this very difficult question in "The Critics' Recognition of an Instance of Literature," *Language and Style*
1 (1968), 243–67.

5. Sometimes the praise is not oblique; it is quite open.
Stanley Edgar Hyman's *The Tangled Bank* (1962; rpt.
New York: Grosset, 1966) treats the works of Darwin, Marx,
Fraser, and Freud "as imaginative organizations, as though
they were poems" (p. ix). The attitudes critics take toward
Darwin's work is especially instructive since he is pre-
eminently the scientist. See, for instance, Theodore Baird's
much-admired essay, "Darwin and the Tangled Bank," *Amer-
ican Scholar* 154 (1946), 477–86. See also the essays by
Walter F. Cannon and A. Dwight Culler in *The Art of*

Victorian Prose, ed. George Levine and William Madden (New York: Oxford University Press, 1968). This last also contains essays on Ruskin's prose by John Rosenberg and on political oratory by John Holloway.

4—The Structure of Fifv

1. The distinction between prose fiction by intention and narrative prose fiction by intention (which, for convenience's sake, I am calling novels) is smudgier, probably, than I have admitted. Perhaps the question is too nice a one to bring into the body of these considerations, but it does deserve some attention. My distinctions are based on such remarks as the following: "All literary works fall into three main classes: poems, essays, and prose fiction. . . . [A] play as read, that is, the script of the play, is a literary work, and falls within our classification; it is either a poem, like *Hamlet,* or a prose fiction, like *Ghosts.*" (Monroe C. Beardsley, *Aesthetics: Problems in the Philosophy of Criticism* [New York: Harcourt, 1958], p. 126.)

But consider the 14 September 1970 issue of *Publishers' Weekly* as suggestive of other uses critics give the word. That issue lists Jorge Luis Borge's *The Book of Imaginary Beings* under nonfiction; I can only suppose that this is because the book lacks a narrative element and that the distinction between narratives and nonnarratives is important. But the same issue also lists Norman Wexler's screenplay for the film *Joe* under nonfiction, and I suppose this must be because it is not a short story, a short novel, or a novel, even though it *does* have a narrative element.

Shall one say, then, that the analysis I have given is inaccurate and that I should say that the word fiction has the meaning 'short stories and novels' and that its next larger meaning is 'all prose fiction by intention except short stories and novels'? A good case might be made for that distinction, or for combining the two; but I have elected to simplify the matter and rely upon Professor Beardsley as more typical of critics than the editors of *Publishers' Weekly.*

This nit-picking does get tiring. Perhaps this is a good

point to remind ourselves that the word fiction is apparently not important at all to some students of literature. The very useful *Annals of English Literature: The Principal Publications of Each Year Together with an Alphabetical Index of Authors with Their Works,* 2nd ed. (Oxford: Clarendon, 1961) manages to get along without using the word fiction as a major label. Its rather curious categories are Prose, Verse, Tragedy, Comedy, and Drama. It thus distinguishes very carefully among three different kinds of plays but lumps all nondramatic prose together. It is still a very useful book.

2. E. M. W. Tillyard and C. S. Lewis, *The Personal Heresy: A Controversy* (1939; rpt. London: Oxford University Press, 1965), pp. 60–61.

3. It is hard to imagine that anyone could get very interested in the matter, but I have explored the possibility that the word fiction is used to refer also to (a) all of imaginative literature and not just that part of it which is admirable, and (b) imaginative literature plus marginal literature as well. The word literature is used with these meanings, for instance, and perhaps the word fiction is also used in these ways. But it seems to me that this does not happen or, at least, that it happens so infrequently that it can be ignored.

4. Graham Hough, *An Essay on Criticism* (New York: Norton, 1966), p. 58. It is worth remarking that he says elsewhere that literature is "a significant fiction" (p. 44).

5. The critics are not alone in their interest in obsolete scientific books nor even, perhaps, first. It is not generally recognized in the humanities, but scientists are beginning to develop a sense of classics in their fields, works that may be obsolete but are still satisfying for human reasons. Apparently, science is slowly gathering a corpus of classics constituting a paraliterature largely unknown to literary critics.

Scientific American is a mine for curious information on the matter of the scientists' literary interest in the classics within their own traditions; see especially its advertising columns and briefer reviews. Dover Publications has had a section in its annual catalogs entitled *Classics of Science,* and other publishers—notably the university presses—show at least sporadic interest in books in this category. An occasional paper or book will give direct attention, but there seems to be no body of opinion and theory emergent as yet. Two papers that take one into the matter in quite different ways are Walter James Miller, "The Classics of Engineering," *College English* 19 (1957), 61–67, and T. L. Cottrell, "The Scientific Textbook as a Work of Art," *A Review of English Literature* (Leeds) 3, No. 4 (October 1962), 7–16. Cottrell's essay argues that scientific books have no interest whatsoever after their contents have been absorbed into the scientific activities of their fields—but old scientific books do get reprinted and sold.

The rise of the history of science as a distinct discipline is no doubt connected with this phenomenon, but whether this is producing the interest or is itself a product of that interest is difficult to say. Some sense of proprietorship has already emerged, however. See Walter F. Cannon, "Darwin's Vision in *On the Origin of Species*," in *The Art of Victorian Prose*, ed. George Levine and William Madden (New York: Oxford University Press, 1968), pp. 154–73, which will show the critic (to his very great delight) that "literary criticism as practised by professors of English literature at liberal arts colleges is not of much importance in understanding the important books of the world since 1859" (p. 173).

6. Albert C. Baugh et al., eds., *A Literary History of England* (New York: Appleton, 1948), p. 1087.

7. Wilbur Sanders, "History and Literary Criticism," *Critical Review* 9 (1966), 118–32.

Critics are aware of this view of science, but they are more likely to have the older view. I suspect this helps explain why it is that the critic is more likely to see similarities between novels and bad-history books than between novels and obsolete-history books: perhaps it is easier to see that the writer of a bad-history book did invent the structures he offers his readers? The writer of a obsolete-history book still seems to us to have "found" much of what he tells us; the writers of legends and of absurdities of natural philosophy seem more obviously to have invented what they tell us and we are the readier to accept their books under the label fiction.

5 – Fiction as Genres

1. M. M. Liberman and Edward E. Foster, *A Modern Lexicon of Literary Terms* (Glenview, Illinois: Scott Foresman, 1968), p. 26. See the entries for *Convention* and *Genre* in this very useful little book.

I go into this matter of genres much more carefully in a paper that refers to them as *grames* and suggests that they are entities having the same general character as do languages and games. In that paper I also suggest that at least three different types of literary grames might be distinguished: form-grames, personality-grames and subject-grames. (See "The Critics' Conception of Literature," *College English* 31 [1969], 1–24.) No satisfactory metataxonomy of literary grames has yet been made, but apparently the grames critics associate with the word fiction are all form grames. I have used the word genre in this book to save elaborate explanations and defenses of the word grame, but I do feel obliged to remark that the word genre has become so very unclear and at the same time so very familiar that its use is hampering thought about fundamental questions in literary theory.

7 – Some Further Queries

1. Joseph Conrad, "Preface to *The Nigger of the 'Narcissus,'* " quoted in Philip Stevick, *The Theory of the Novel* (New York: Free Press, 1967), p. 399.

2. Erich Auerbach, *Mimesis: The Representation of Reality in Western Literature*, trans. Willard Trask (1953; rpt. New York: Doubleday, 1957), p. 450.

3. Irving Howe, "Mass Society and Post-Modern Fiction," reprinted in *Approaches to the Novel*, ed. Robert Scholes (San Francisco: Chandler, 1961), pp. 282–83.

4. This is so common a charge that it hardly needs documentation. A good example is Henri Peyre's characterization of the novels of Louis-Ferdinand Celine in *French Novelists of Today* (New York: Oxford University Press, 1967), especially pp. 187–95.

5. "Lyric. Originally a song accompanied by a lyre; now used to refer not only to the words of a song but also to brief song-like poems not necessarily written to be sung, short meditative poems that express personal emotions, and several more complex and elaborate structures." Herbert Goldstone and Irving Cummings, eds., *Poets & Poems* (Belmont, Calif.: Wadsworth, 1967), p. 389.

6. Richard Freedman calls *The Great Gatsby* "the greatest American poem" in "The Well-Read Reader," *Book World*, 31 October 1971, 5. Stanley Edgar Hyman treats Darwin's book as a poem in *The Tangled Bank* (New York: Grosset, 1962).

7. E. E. Evans-Pritchard, *Social Anthropology and Other Essays* (1962; rptd. New York: Free Press, 1964), pp. 46–47. Professor Evans-Pritchard is here explaining the attitudes of diffusionist anthropologists and is not referring to fiction in any sense.

Oscar Wilde put it another way: "Who he was who first, without ever having gone out to the rude chase, told the wondering cavemen at sunset how he had dragged the Megatherium from the purple darkness of its jasper cave, or slain the Mammoth in single combat and brought back its gilded tusks, we cannot tell, and not one of our modern anthropologists, for all their much-boasted science, has had the ordinary courage to tell us." "The Decay of Lying," from *Intentions*, in *The Complete Works of Oscar Wilde* (Garden City, N. Y.: Doubleday, 1923), 5: 34.

8. Paul Radin and James Johnson Sweeney, eds., *African Folktales and Sculpture* (New York: Pantheon, 1952), p. 12.

9. Lu Hsun gives *hsiao-shuo* as the Chinese equivalent for the word fiction and shows that this originally meant 'small talk' or 'chitchat,' for instance. His history makes it seem very doubtful that the word fiction does translate neatly into *hsiao-shuo* very often. See A *Brief History of Chinese Fiction*, trans. Yang Hsien-Yi and Gladys Yang, China Knowledge Series (Peking: Foreign Language Press, 1959), especially pp. 1–23.

10. William Bascom reports that the Ojibwa is "to my knowledge the only society reported to lack fictional prose

narratives." It may be that this is the case, but so many of the reports field anthropologists have given of "myths," "legends," and "fiction" are so casual in their distinctions among those categories and not infrequently glib in their explanations of them that it seems to me the question may still be open. Many anthropologists, I suspect, are importing into the cultures they are studying those literary distinctions our own culture has programmed into them. See William Bascom, "The Forms of Folklore: Prose Narratives," *Journal of American Folklore* 78 (1965), especially p. 16 and footnote citation.

Glossary

There are only ten terms to be explained and so I have chosen to arrange them in a logical rather than in an alphabetical sequence. It should be remembered that each term has two meanings; it refers to a class of texts and also to a class of genres. The brief definitions given here will serve as reminders for those who have already studied the full explanations in the text, but some of these definitions cannot be understood unless one has studied the whole of the explanations.

It has proven impossible to list examples of genres which are members of the various subclasses. The entire area of genre theory remains tantalizingly mysterious; it is a mass of confusion shot through with many brilliant insights and overlaid with various conflicting quasi systems. There is no generally accepted catalogue of genres, and I have decided that cowardice is the wiser policy here. I have confined myself to lists of the texts typically associated with the various classes.

1. The three major classes:

1a. *Fifv.* All books and genres that are fiction by intention or fiction by value or both.

Fifv is the superclass containing all meanings critics normally give the word fiction. The counterclass to fifv might be called *never-fiction*; no book or genre in this counterclass would ever be named fiction in the normal critical usage of the word.

1b. *Fiction by intention.* A book is fiction by intention if its writer has knowingly made it factually untrue but also warned his readers he has done this. A genre is fiction by intention if among its rules is the stipulation that books produced within its tradition meet the description just given.

Texts associated with fiction by intention include both good and bad novels and short stories but also good and bad verse and all nonnarrative prose that is fiction by intention. Texts not associated with the class are good and bad works of history, great works in verse that are not fiction by intention, scientific works, and so forth.

Extracritical uses of the word fiction (when the word is not used to mean 'untruth') are apparently confined to this one large class of meanings.

1c. *Fiction by value.* All books and genres which deserve to be deeply admired. This is coterminous with the class *great books*, but it is subdivided in a unique and important way.

The texts associated with this class are the great works of any origin and are not confined to, say, verse and plays and fiction by intention. Texts typically not associated with the class are bad novels and short stories, verse which has only mnemonic purposes, commercial theater, undistinguished scientific books, and the like.

2. Three subclasses found in both fiction by intention and fiction by value:

2a. *Great novels.* All books and genres which are great prose narrative fiction by intention.

Note that the texts associated with this class include more than the novel per se. They typically include Fielding's *Tom Jones* (a novel), Hawthorne's *Scarlet Letter* (a romance), Melville's *Billy Budd* (a short novel), Chekhov's "The Kiss" (a short story), Shaw's *Man and Superman* (a play). These are the narrowest meanings the word fiction has in normal critical usage, though there may be infrequent occasions on which it refers to only the great novels proper. These are the most important meanings the word has: they appear in all the other meanings.

2b. *Great prose fiction by intention.* All books and genres which deserve to be deeply admired, are in prose, and are fiction by intention.

Texts typically associated with these classes are all those listed under great novels and also all nonnarrative works, like Peter Finley Dunne's *Mr. Dooley's Philosophy*, which do not have a narrative thread but are fiction by intention and in prose and admirable. These classes wholly contain great novels.

2c. *Great fiction by intention.* All books in prose or verse, and all genres, which are admirable and are fiction by intention.

Texts typically associated with these classes are those listed as great prose fiction by intention but also such works as Coleridge's "The Ancient Mariner," which is not prose but is a great work and is fiction by intention. These classes wholly contain great prose fiction by intention.

3. Three classes which extend out of fiction by value into fiction by intention:

3a. *Novels.* All books and all genres, regardless of merit, which are narrative and are prose and are fiction by intention.

Texts typically associated with these classes are all those listed as great novels but also such novels and short stories and plays in prose as are not considered admirable: Jacqueline Susann's *The Valley of the Dolls*, O. Henry's "The Gift of the Magi," and so forth. These classes wholly contain great novels.

3b. *Prose fiction by intention.* All books and all genres, regardless of merit, which are prose and also fiction by intention.

Texts typically associated with these classes are those listed under novels but also include nonnarrative works, like Dunne's *Mr. Dooley's Philosophy*, whether they are admirable or not. These classes wholly contain great prose fiction by intention and also novels.

3c. *Fiction by intention.* These classes have already been defined: see 1b. Included in them are all prose fiction by intention and also all verse fiction by intention, regardless of merit.

4. Three classes which extend out of fiction by intention into fiction by value:

4a. *Great imaginative literature.* All books, and all genres, which are fiction by intention or verse (or both) and which are admirable; also, all plays and dramatic genres which are great are in these classes.

Texts typically associated with these classes are those listed for great fiction by intention but also such works as are not fiction by intention as Milton's *Paradise Lost* and Shakespeare's *Julius Caesar.* These classes wholly include great fiction by intention and represent the most restricted senses in which critics use the word *literature.*

4b. *Great literature.* A book is great literature if it deserves to be deeply admired and it is either (a) a play or in verse or fiction by intention or (b) in one of the less central literary kinds (e.g., the personal essay) or (c) it is in one of the nonliterary kinds and has come to be thought of in that kind as either bad or obsolete. A genre is great literature if it deserves to be deeply admired and (a) is one of those which produce plays, verse, or fiction by intention or (b) is one of the less central literary kinds or (c) is one of the nonliterary kinds (e.g., natural history writing) now come to be thought of within the discipline of which it is a part as bad or as obsolete. Conversely, any great book or genre which is not thought of as primarily the property of a nonliterary discipline is great literature.

Texts typically associated with these classes are all those associated with great imaginative literature but also such books as Boswell's *Life of Johnson* (biography) and Darwin's *Origin of Species* (now becoming obsolete as biology). These classes wholly include great imaginative literature and represent the broadest senses critics commonly give the word literature.

4c. *Fiction by value.* These classes have already been defined; see 1c. They include all great books and great genres, the nonliterary as well as the literary.

Bibliographical Note

In this book I present a theory of fictionality and a theory of the relations the concept of fiction has with the concepts of poetry and drama and literature, the whole amounting to a theory of the structure of the critical mentality. The footnotes offer advice to anyone wanting to explore for himself most of the questions I touch on, but the theory of the concept-structures in criticism and the theory of fictionality call for additional and separate treatment. A mere enumeration of books studied will be of little use to the reader, but perhaps some general reflections on other work done in these two areas will save him trouble.

1. *Fictionality*. A concern about fictionality—and especially about the relationships between truth and fiction—is already evident in Aristotle's *Poetics*. It is useful to distinguish three groups who have given special attention to the matter: the novelists, the philosophers, and the literary critics. A fourth group—a new generation of folklorists—has only recently become interested.

I suppose it should not surprise any of us to learn that practicing novelists have the least help to give anyone who wants to explore the most general questions about fictionality with any very high degree of rigor. We do not normally turn to comedians for rigorous theories of comedy, and I suppose we should not expect novelists to turn from novel-making to the quite different activity of theory-making. Novelists write about fiction and about truth in their prefaces, in their letters and journals, and in their reviews of the work of other writers. Any collection of their observations is a mine for curious data about their motivations and their own understandings (and misunderstandings) of their books but it is only indirectly useful when we want answers to the kinds of questions I consider here.

They must be read, however. What they say severely tests any answers one may think one has found. Two very good collections of novelists' remarks are Miriam Allott, *Novelists on the Novel* (1959; rpt. New York: Columbia University Press, 1966) and Howard E. Hugo, *Aspects of Fiction: A Handbook* (Boston: Little, Brown, 1962). (The most obvious difference between my own theories of fictionality and those of the novelists and critics is that I have not concerned myself with what is their chief preoccupation: the attempt to distinguish theoretically between good fiction and bad. In that connection, see the most eminent of all novelist-theoreticians, Henry James, especially in Richard Blackmur's edition of his prefaces, *The Art of the Novel* [New York: Scribners, 1934].)

The philosopher is concerned about certain logical problems posed by fictional sentences, and much of what he says bears directly upon the matters I take up here. But there is a difference: I am chiefly interested in certain categories of recognition found in literary criticism (what do *critics* accept as fiction? as true? why?), and I have found I had to go outside the philosophical tradition if I was to find the answers I needed.

One book has been particularly helpful to me, and I strongly urge that critics who find aesthetics wearisome get to know Monroe C. Beardsley's *Aesthetics: Problems in the Philosophy of Criticism* (New York: Harcourt, 1958). I had already formed my own (similar) theory of fictionality before reading *Aesthetics*, but I found it immensely rewarding anyway. See especially pages 419–37, 441–43, and 446–47 for a good introduction to the philosophers' discussion of the relations between truth and fiction. A characteristic treatment in a somewhat older philosophical tradition—one many critics will find more congenial—is John Hospers, *Meaning and Truth in the Arts* (Chapel Hill, N. C.: University of North Carolina, 1946). Many short essays in the philosophical journals are missed at the critic's peril; see, for instance, F. E. Sparshott, "Truth in Fiction," *JAAC* 26 (1967), 3–7, for the definitive solution of a problem still giving working critics difficulty.

It may well be that in times to come historians of literary criticism will speak of the 1960s as the period when every critic gave his attention to the theory of fiction. Until the publication of Wayne C. Booth's *Rhetoric of Fiction* (Chicago: University of Chicago Press, 1961), by far the bulk of everything written about fiction by literary critics in this century had been devoted to the interpretation and praise of individual works and individual writers. Given a week or two, someone interested in reading the best theorizing critics had done could have worked through Percy Lubbock, E. M. Forster, Edwin Muir, Joseph Warren Beach and one or two others, and then legitimately claimed that he had read just about everything important. But so much good work has been done since 1960 that it is far, far different now.

Anyone seeking a good overview of critical inquiry into fiction will most wisely begin with René Wellek and Austin Warren, "The Nature and Modes of Narrative Fiction," *Theory of Literature*, 3rd ed. (New York: Harcourt, 1962), pp. 212–25. He will learn that critics ask themselves these questions: "What are the different kinds of fiction?" "Which is the best kind of fiction?" "Which is the best kind of novel?" "Why is fiction so important to humanity?" (This last question begs some prior questions, but it is the only form queries into the value of fiction take in criticism.) I find no evidence of a disinterested concern about the boundaries between fiction and not-fiction.

Robert Scholes and Robert Kellogg, *The Nature of Narrative* (New York: Oxford University Press, 1966), gives a very good introduction to the variety of kinds of fiction recognized. Northrop Frye's *The Anatomy of Criticism* (Princeton: Princeton University Press, 1957) is so well known it might be forgotten here: it offers its own typology of fiction. There are several collections of essays on problems connected with the novel. The best, I think, is the one done by my friend Philip Stevick, *The Theory of the Novel* (New York: Free Press, 1967). Booth's *The Rhetoric of Fiction* should be known to anyone who has any interest at all in these matters. It does not address itself to the questions I consider in this essay, but it does offer instant sophistication in the fiction criticism of our time, and it is a delightful book to read. Even the briefest bibliographical note ought to mention two other studies: Ian Watt's *The Rise of the Novel*: *Studies in Defoe, Richardson and Fielding* (Berkeley, Calif.: University of California Press, 1957), a fine representative of the tradition of historical studies in fiction, and Erich Auerbach's *Mimesis*: *The Representation of Reality in Western Literature*, trans. Willard Trask (Princeton, N. J.: Princeton University Press, 1953), a splendidly readable account of many matters I hardly touch on here.

No list of fiction studies that fails to include reference to such historical investigation as that of Ernest Baker and, say, Richard Stang, to the novel-criticism of Dorothy Van Ghent and Georg Lukács, to the contributions men like Bernard Russell and H. Vaihinger have made to the theory of fiction, and to the more recent work of David Lodge and of Frank Kermode and of Dorothy Walsh can claim to offer more than the simplest introduction to the field. But there already are several good bibliographies of fiction studies that will serve the serious investigator.

The following seem especially worth knowing about: the bibliographies in Wellek and Warren, *Theory of Literature*, for their reference to European studies; the "Notes" in Scholes and Kellogg, *The Nature of Narrative*, which cite many works (e.g., that of Delehaye on hagiography) neglected by literary critics; the "Notes and Queries" sections in Beardsley's *Aesthetics*—not only because they refer one to the work that has appeared in the philosophical journals but because they give one an intelligent preview of it; Bradford A. Booth's essay, "The Novel," in *Contemporary Literary Scholarship*: *A Critical Review*, ed. Lewis Leary (New York: Appleton, 1958) as a particularly useful introduction to historical scholarship for the newcomer; and, finally, the long, annotated bibliographies of Booth's *Rhetoric of Fiction* and Stevick's *Theory of the Novel*.

One last remark: students of folklore have recently begun
to show keen interest in the kinds of theoretical discussions
covered here, and they are worth reading because they de-
provincialize one about the forms fiction may take. A very
good start into the literature can be made with William
Bascom, "The Forms of Folklore: Prose Narratives," *Journal of American Folklore* 78 (1965), 3–20.

II. *The structure of the critical mentality.* This book pro-
poses a theory that the basic terminology of literary critics —
which we have always known is ambiguous — is ambiguous in
intensely and symmetrically patterned ways. So far as I
know, there has been no other attempt quite like it to identify concept-structures in the critical mentality, but everything critics have written about literature in general and
about the words they use is relevant in one way or another.

Where does one turn if one wants to know how critics
normally use words like drama and literature and fiction?
The general dictionaries are not very helpful, and so one
turns to the glossaries of literary terminology. But these do
not offer much help either if the term is in very common
use in criticism and one wants sophisticated information.
The glossaries now available are excellent, but they are all in
the rare-word tradition in lexicography; they are precisely
what one needs if one wants to remind oneself of what
T. S. Eliot meant when he used the phrase *objective correla-
tive* or what the rhetorical figure *hendiadys* is, but they are
blank or merely reverential when it comes to words like
poetry and fiction. One really cannot fault them for this,
because words like fiction offer very special problems in objective definition. The uses a basic term is given are immensely subtle and sophisticated, and they do not reveal
themselves within the scope of any single sentence in which
they appear. Further, people disagree violently on which
uses are proper and deserve to be recognized in glossaries
and which, though common, are improper and ought to be
ignored. Not surprisingly, the literary glossaries avoid the
problem, and they will continue to avoid it until special
studies of those terms have been made.

But the glossaries now available really are splendidly helpful in many ways, and these are the ones I found myself turning to again and again as I followed out the many false and true clues that eventually led me to the theory I present: W. V. Ruttkowski and R. E. Blake, *Glossary of Literary Terms in English, German and French with Greek and Latin Derivations of Terms for the Student of General and Comparative Literature* (Bern: Francke Verlag, 1969); Joseph T. Shipley, ed. *Dictionary of World Literary Terms*, 3rd ed. (Boston: The Writer, 1970); Alex Preminger et al., *Encyclopedia of Poetry and Poetics* (Princeton, N. J.: Princeton University Press, 1965); William Flint Thrall, Addison Hibbard, and C. Hugh Holman, *A Handbook to Literature*, 2nd ed. (New York: Odyssey, 1960); and Henri Morier, *Dictionnaire de poétique et de rhétorique* (Paris: Presses Universitaires de France, 1961).

Since the word fiction is often used as a synonym for the word literature, all speculations on literature are (in principle) relevant to this theory. But that covers an area which is bounded on one side by, say, Gertrude Stein's delightful "Descriptions of Literature," in *transition: An International Quarterly for Creative Experiment* No. 13 (Summer 1928), pp. 50–53—amateur theorizing at its finest—and on the other by Knut Hanneborg's awesomely scholarly *The Study of Literature: A Contribution to the Phenomenology of the Humane Sciences* (Oslo: Universitetsforlaget, 1967), which is a very difficult book to read but deserves serious attention. Wellek and Warren, "The Nature of Literature," in *Theory of Literature*, pp. 20–28, 321–23, gives a good introduction to the full range of that speculation.

Finally, the reader newly wandered into this area ought to be warned that all the work philosophers and critics now do on the meanings of terms gives either explicit or implicit recognition to the work of Ludwig Wittgenstein as it appears in his *Philosophical Investigations*, trans. G. E. M. Anscombe (Oxford: Blackwell, 1958). It would be unwise for anyone to go into these matters who does not have some acquaintance with that book.

Index

truth, 24–25; as indicator of fiction by intention, 110–11

Sudanese and fiction by intention, 10, 104, 107

Sue Barton stories, ix

Supreme achievement, the phrase, 44

Susann, Jacqueline: *The Valley of the Dolls*, 8, 34, 61, 62, 123; *The Love Machine*, 49; mentioned, 9

Swahili epic, 38

Syllables, invention of new, x

Tale, the term, 24

Taste, literary: its complexity, 37

Tastes in foods: incoherent diversity, 36–37

Television cue cards, undisguised reading of: as fiction by intention performance, 105

Terminology: and work of Ludwig Wittgenstein, 130

Texts: distinguished from genres, 2, 73–76

Thackeray, William Makepeace: "Pocahontas," 8, 34; *Vanity Fair*, 58, 109; mentioned, 9, 60

Theory, literary: justification, x–xi

"Thirty Days Hath Steptember," 48, 98

Thousand and One Nights, The, 50

Tolkien, J. R. R., 11

Tolstoy, Leo: *War and Peace*, 5; *Anna Karenina*, 8, 9, 10, 11, 18, 34, 39, 49, 69; *The Death of Ivan Ilyich*, 58; mentioned, 9

Tom Swift novels, 76

Topographical poem: the genre, 75

Tradition, the term, 74

Traditions, literary and non-literary, 67–71

Traven, B.: *Bridge in the Jungle*, 35, 43, 84

True Confessions, 25

True Story, 25

Truth: of history, 11, and generality and factuality, 11–12; and fiction by intention, 14–15; factual and propositional, 19–21; and novels, 87–90

Truth in sentences: to reality, 28; to their source, 30–31

Twain, Mark (Clemens, Samuel L.): *Huckleberry Finn*, 8, 34, 49; mentioned, 9

Unread books thought admirable: importance to fiction by value, 37–38

Untruth: factual, and fiction by intention, 12–15; factual, and books, 19; factual, and propositional, 19–21; as meaning for word *fiction*, 122. *See also* Truth in sentences

Valtin, Jan (Richard Krebs): *Out of the Night*, 25

Verse: defined, 48; identical with poetry by intention, 99; characterized, 99–100; mentioned, 100

Verse and poetry distinguished, 48

Verse narrative fiction by intention: a counterclass to novels, 53

Verse/prose distinction: and fiction by intention, 9; discussed, 48

Vers libre, 48

Walpole, Horace, 66